Multimedia Presentation Technology

THE WADSWORTH

MIS

SERIES

The Wadsworth Series in Management Information Systems

Applying Expert System Technology to Business, Patrick Lyons
Business Systems Analysis and Design, William S. Davis
Database Systems: Design, Implementation, and Management, Peter Rob and Carlos Coronel
Intelligent Systems for Business: Expert Systems with Neural Networks, Fatemeh Zahedi
Microcomputers for Managers, Bay Arinze
Multimedia Presentation Technology, Fred T. Hofstetter
Networks in Action: Business Choices and Telecommunications Decisions, Peter G.W. Keen and
J. Michael Cummins
The New Software Engineering, Sue Conger

Forthcoming Titles
Development of Quality Multimedia, Donald Carpenter
Information Technology in a Global Business Environment: Readings and Cases, P. Candace Deans and
Jaak Jurison
Information Technology in Action, Peter G. W. Keen
Human Resources for Information Managers, Pamela K. D'Huyvetter
Local Area Networks with Novell, H. Rene Baca, Christopher M. Zager, and Margaret A. Zinky
Management Handbook of Multimedia, Antone F. Alber
Managing Quality Information Systems, Fatemeh Zahedi
MIS Classics, Peter G. W. Keen and Lynda Keen
Rapid Software Deployment: An Object-oriented Approach to End-user Computing, Ali Bahrami

Fred T. Hofstetter
University of Delaware

Multimedia Presentation Technology

with a Sample Presentation on Total Quality Management

Includes Tutorial Copies of PODIUM for DOS,
PODIUM for Windows, and PODIUM for
OS/2 Presentation Manager

Wadsworth Publishing Company
Belmont, California
A Division of Wadsworth, Inc.

Publisher: Kathy Shields
Editorial Assistant: Tamara Huggins
Multimedia Project Manager: Pat Waldo
Managing Designer: Andrew Ogus
Print Buyer: Randy Hurst
Permissions Editor: Peggy Meehan
Cover and Interior Designer: Peter Martin/Design Office
Copy Editor: Rebecca Magee
Cover Photograph: © Bernard Roussel/Image Bank
Signing Representative: Ron Shelly
Compositor: Wadsworth Digital Productions
Printer: Banta

This book is printed on acid-free recycled paper.

International Thomson Publishing
The trademark ITP is used under license.

Printed in the United States of America

1 2 3 4 5 6 7 8 9 10—98 97 96 95 94

ISBN 0-534-20676-X

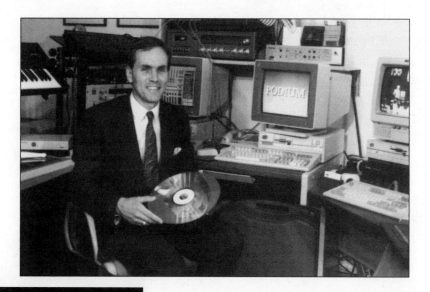

ABOUT THE AUTHOR

F red T. Hofstetter was born and raised in Columbus, Ohio. A graduate of Saint Joseph's College and The Ohio State University, Dr. Hofstetter is director of the Instructional Technology Center at the University of Delaware. A specialist in multimedia computing for music composition, desktop publishing, interactive video, digital television, compact disc, hand-held scanning, computer-based instruction, and classroom media projection, he developed the PODIUM hypermedia program for DOS, Windows, and OS/2 Presentation Manager. A full professor of music and education, he authored the *GUIDO Ear-Training Lessons*, *Making Music on Micros*, and *Computer Literacy for Musicians*.

A recipient of many grants and awards, Dr. Hofstetter also does consulting work for computer firms. He founded the Association for Technology in Music Instruction and has published in the *Journal of Computer-Based Instruction*, *Journal of Research in Music Educa-*

tion, College Music Symposium, Music Educators Journal, Electronic Learning, Creative Computing, Technological Horizons in Education, and *Tech Trends.* He has given lectures and workshops on computers and music in many locations in Europe, Africa, Australia, Canada, the United States, and the Pacific Rim. Dr. Hofstetter is the principal investigator of the *Videodisc Music Series,* funded by the National Endowment for the Humanities and winner of a gold CINDY award.

As one of the world's most heavily traveled multimedia presenters, Dr. Hofstetter shares with you twenty years of experience that have enabled him to contribute the many tips, caveats, suggestions, and helpful checklists this book provides.

TABLE OF CONTENTS

PART ONE

Behind the Scenes   2

Primer   55

PART THREE

Implementation   154

Successful people will tell you that one of their most important attributes is the ability to communicate persuasively. That is why no matter what profession you have chosen, presentation technology can help you be more effective. Teachers can transform the classroom from a dull and lifeless chalk dust atmosphere into an engaging multimedia environment rich in color imagery, full-motion video, and stereo sound. Business executives can have instant access to corporate information, product illustrations, and up-to-the-minute charts and graphs of company data. Marketing reps can use a multimedia sales portfolio to woo potential clients, with instant access to full-color product illustrations, sound bites, and motion video clips. Government officials can use direct-to-disk digital video recording technology to document current events and safeguard our national interests.

If you have ever seen a multimedia presentation, you were probably impressed with how it moved the audience. Indeed, the interplay of full-color imaging, digital audio, full-motion video, and stereo sound provides a powerful way to captivate an audience and get your message across. You probably wish you could use multimedia and be so successful in your own presentations. But do you feel that you really can do it yourself? That is what this book is about; it will empower you to make your own presentations and become a master of multimedia.

This book has three parts. Part One introduces the basic principles of presentation technology that will help you understand what presentation technology is, what it can do, and what you should expect from presentation software programs. Multimedia has a lot of glitz that makes it look harder than it really is. A bit of background knowledge will help you understand why making multimedia presentations need not be so complicated that you must hire someone to produce them for you. Having to rely on an outside production house removes the immediacy of being able to produce timely creations that will make your presentations relevant to the needs of your students, the turn of current events, or the last minute pressures of your business.

Part Two contains a tutorial that applies these principles to the production of an actual multimedia presentation. You can either take an arm's length or hands-on approach to this tutorial. If you prefer to read through it without actually completing the exercises, the arm's length approach will give you a good overview of what is involved in creating a multimedia presentation; then you can decide whether you want to get personally involved with presentation technology.

On the other hand, if you have an IBM-compatible personal computer with VGA graphics and 2 MB or more of RAM, you can use the presentation software that comes with this book to work through the exercises and create an actual multimedia presentation. This book comes with a CD-ROM that contains a tutorial copy of the PODIUM presentation software along with a collection of multimedia materials used in the tutorial. Instructions for using the PODIUM CD-ROM can be found at the beginning of Part Two. If your computer does not have a CD-ROM drive, the instructions tell how to transfer the materials onto diskettes that can be used with your computer.

The topic of the tutorial is Total Quality Management (TQM). In addition to showing how to build a presentation, the tutorial contains practical suggestions for using the TQM process to improve business productivity and educational effectiveness.

After you complete the tutorial and realize how easily you can create your own multimedia presentations, you will want to know how to equip yourself and your school, company, or agency to deliver them. Part Three covers these logistics by providing you with an implementation guide that shows how to equip existing facilities, plan for new construction, and make multimedia portable. Checklists for each setup will help you avoid oversights and needless expense. Tips for scanning text, digitizing slides, and recording digital video and audio will guide you in the creation of multimedia objects. Catalogs, indexes, magazines, resource guides, and multimedia expositions and conferences are listed so you can stay abreast of new developments in this exciting field.

Acknowledgments

This book is dedicated to the thousands of PODIUM users who are applying its principles of multimedia presentation technology to improve teaching effectiveness, business productivity, military preparedness, and government responsiveness. The author wishes to recognize their ongoing suggestions for enhancements and new features that make PODIUM evolve according to user needs. In particular, the author wishes to thank the following people:

- Brenda Boccard of Florida Community College at Jacksonville
- Annette Billie of Fayetteville State University
- Wayne Debly of Humber College
- Jack Edwards of Webster Elementary School
- Pat Fox of Trident Technical College
- Charles and Mary Ruth Hassett of Fort Hays State University
- Paul Jacobsen of Western Nebraska Community College
- James Johnson of Oklahoma City Community College
- John McFadden of Loyola College
- Brian McGuire of Northeast Missouri State University
- Sue Michael of the University of Kentucky
- Iain Miller of Wright State University
- Thomas Panek of APT Corporation
- Michael Pearson of West Chester University
- Ed Pinheiro of IBM Corporation
- Carol Race of Northeast Missouri State University
- Bob Romanoff of the National Institutes of Health
- Christine Russell of the College of DuPage
- Art Shmarak of the University of California Davis School of Medicine
- Dean Zollman of Kansas State University.

As the host institution at which this book was written, the University of Delaware continues to provide an environment conducive to the research and development of technological innovations. Dean Frank B. Murray is a valued friend and mentor. The author is particularly grateful to the staff of the Instructional Technology Center; Dave Anderer, Chris Brooks, Morris Brooks, Janet Harbaugh, Mike Morgan, George Mulford, Pat Sine, Kathie Troutman, and James Wilson have made important contributions that include teaching PODIUM seminars, consulting with users, creating brochures, providing technical advice, and testing the tutorial part of this book. From Computing and Network Services, George Harding provided invaluable assistance with multimedia hardware issues, and Steve Timmins contributed to the section on animation.

In 1988, Joe Melloy of IBM Corporation suggested the name PODIUM, and over a couple of beers, helped the author brainstorm how it could become an acronym (Presentation Overlay Display for Interactive Uses of Media). Later that year, Professor Paul Sammelwitz of the University of Delaware's College of Agricultural Sciences entered his lesson plans and lecture notes into PODIUM before anyone else realized it would let you do that; this had a profound impact on the future development of the PODIUM user interface, and Paul continues to be a valued friend, user, and adviser.

Very special thanks is due Laura Hofstetter, the author's wife, who not only provided moral support for this project, but also rendered the Total Quality Management bitmaps on the CD-ROM included with this book. No one could be a better friend or partner than Laura.

Fred T. Hofstetter

Multimedia
Presentation
Technology

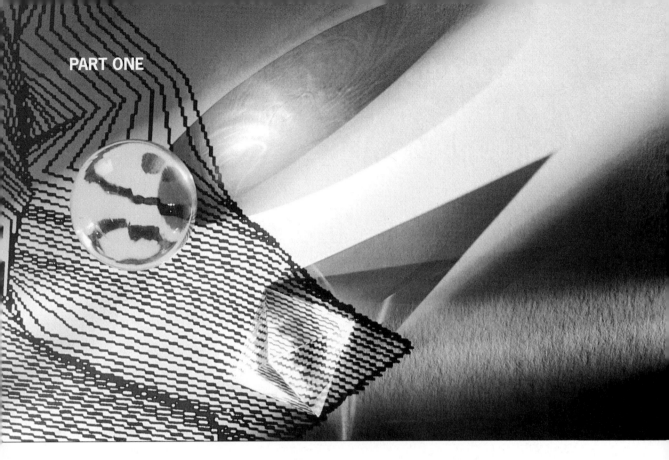

This book is based on eight principles that define a multimedia presentation system. Chapters 1 through 8 present these principles; learning them will help you understand how you can make your own multimedia presentations quickly and easily. The principles will empower you to

1 flow any text onto your screen to create beautifully typeset slides in the font of your choice;

2 link any line of text to any other text, providing you with split-second access to any slide at any time;

3 put any picture on your computer screen, including 35-mm slides, flat art, video, computer graphics, and clip art;

4 make any part of any picture a hot spot that can trigger a link to any object on your computer or network;

5 think of the text files, pictures, waveform audio files, animation sequences, digital video files, and application programs on your computer as objects that can be linked;

Behind the Scenes

6 link any multimedia object to any combination of multimedia objects, including color images, audio sound tracks, and full-motion video;

7 use metaphors that make multimedia easy to understand yet infinitely powerful to use; and

8 adopt standards that will help you minimize costs, save time, and maximize your gain from using multimedia.

Presentation software programs without these capabilities make using multimedia more difficult, more time-consuming, and more expensive than it needs to be. They also restrict your movement through your materials during a presentation, limiting the level of interactivity you can have to respond to the needs of the moment, and thereby hampering your effectiveness.

Chapter 1

Flowing Text into Slides

Y ou can take any text and flow it beautifully onto the screen in the style of your choice. You can create this text yourself with any text editor or word processor, or you can use text that has already been word processed. The only requirement is that the text be stored as ASCII characters. *ASCII* stands for American Standard Code for Information Interchange and is the standard way characters are stored inside a computer. Almost every word processor contains an option for saving files in the ASCII format.

Consider the text file illustrated in Figure 1.1; it contains three sentences. When flowed onto the screen using a "clustered" style, it appears carefully typeset, as shown in Figure 1.2. Notice how each sentence appears as a cluster marked with a bullet. In Part Two of this book, you learn how to flow text onto the screen using several different styles. For now, just focus on this principle: Any ASCII text file can quickly and easily become a beautifully typeset slide in your presentation.

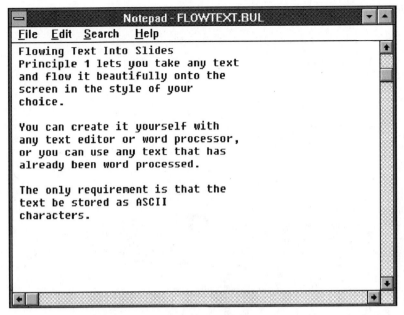

FIGURE 1.1
An ASCII text file of information as displayed by a text editor.

Lesson Plans and Course Outlines

Many teachers and faculty members already have their course outlines and lesson plans word processed. Because any text can be flowed onto the screen in any font, these educators have a head start making multimedia presentations.

Using the hypertext and hypermedia principles discussed later in this book, teachers can make links between course objectives, lesson plans, and audiovisual materials needed for class. This can be done with any text editor, making class preparation quick and easy. Because text files require little space on a computer, teachers can literally have instant access to all of their course outlines and lesson plans at once.

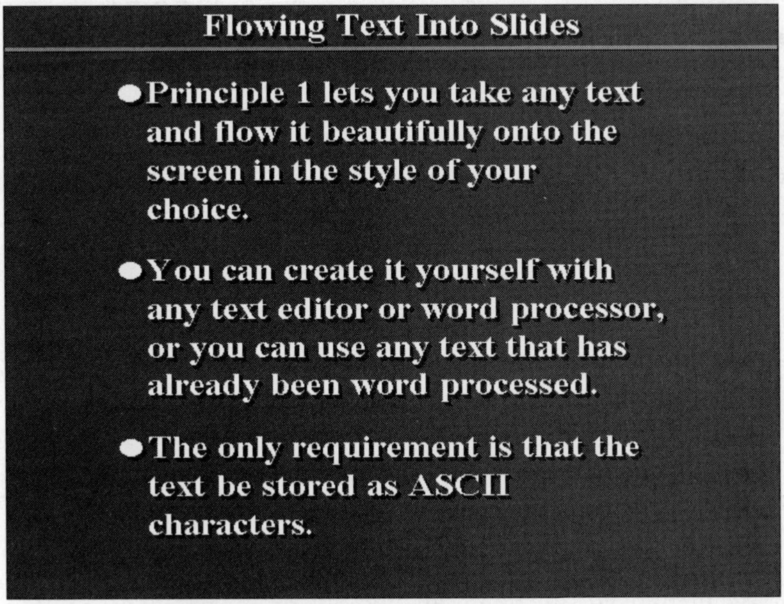

Flowing Text Into Slides

- Principle 1 lets you take any text and flow it beautifully onto the screen in the style of your choice.

- You can create it yourself with any text editor or word processor, or you can use any text that has already been word processed.

- The only requirement is that the text be stored as ASCII characters.

FIGURE 1.2
How the text in Figure 1.1 appears when flowed onto the screen in a clustered style.

Corporate Data

Computerization has made corporations information-rich. A fortunate by-product is that virtually all of this information is available in machine-readable form that can be flowed onto the computer screen quickly and easily for use in presentations. This includes corporate policy manuals, training materials, phone books, sales histories, customer profiles, and reports. Using the hypertext and hypermedia principles presented in Part One of this book, the user can easily create links among these materials, making it possible to access any corporate data on demand quickly, effectively, and beautifully.

Inventory Lists

For example, a company may wish to provide its sales force with an inventory list on their laptop computers. When a salesperson calls on a customer, the list can be displayed on the laptop screen. As the customer peruses the list and expresses interest in a product, the salesperson can instantly link to pictures of the product, pricing information, and delivery schedules.

Newspaper Articles

As previously mentioned, any text from any source can be used in a presentation graphics program. Even late-breaking news, such as an article in the morning newspaper, can be presented. Low-cost hand-held scanners let the user scan any text into an ASCII file and then have instant access to it during a presentation. This process is so quick and easy that you can even scan materials while interacting with a class of students or a group of customers, and you then have instant access to that material for the rest of your career.

Figure 1.4 shows how the newspaper article in Figure 1.3 flows onto the screen after conversion to ASCII text by a hand-held scanner. No changes were made to the text file after the newspaper article was scanned; it simply was flowed onto the screen in a clustered style.

FRIDAY, JULY 9, 1993 • USA TODAY

'Smart bomb' drug kills cancer in mice

By Anita Manning
USA TODAY

Researchers have cured cancer in mice using what they call a chemical "smart bomb" that seeks and destroys tumors.

Pamela Trail, of the Bristol-Myers Squibb Pharmaceutical Research Center in Princeton, N.J., Thursday said scientists linked a genetically engi-neered antibody to an anti-can-cer drug called doxorubicin.

The result: BR96-DOX, a drug that circulates in the bloodstream, finds cancer and "selectively delivers the anti-cancer agent to tumor cells."

Tests involved up to 400 mice implanted with human lung, colon and breast cancers.

Long-term cures were achieved, Trail says, in 72% to 100% of them, depending on dosages and stage of disease.

Findings are reported in to-day's *Science*. Trail says it's too soon to celebrate discovery of the long-sought "magic bullet" cure, but "we've seen excellent anti-tumor activity – cures of tumors. The proof will come from clinical trials."

Her firm will apply to do hu-man trials within six months.

FIGURE 1.3
A newspaper article that you convert to ASCII text with a hand-held scanner. Copyright 1993, USA TODAY. Reprinted with permission.

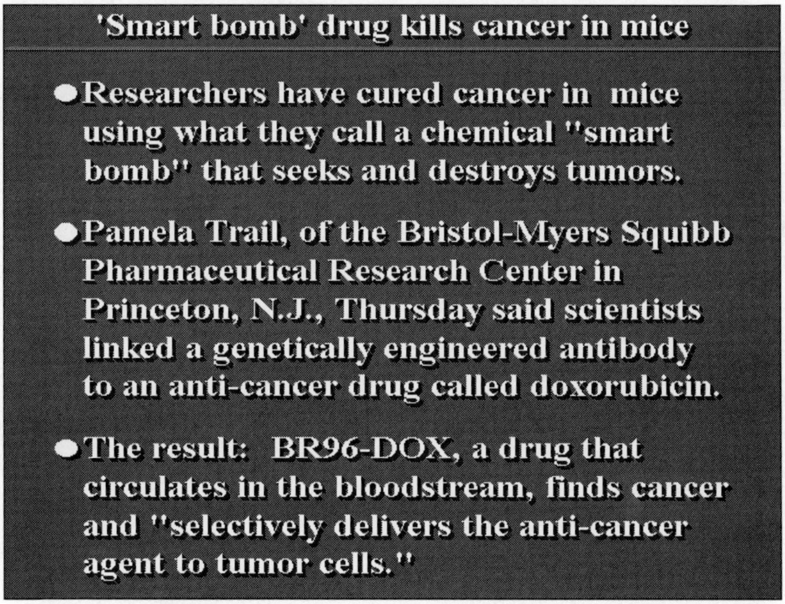

'Smart bomb' drug kills cancer in mice

- Researchers have cured cancer in mice using what they call a chemical "smart bomb" that seeks and destroys tumors.

- Pamela Trail, of the Bristol-Myers Squibb Pharmaceutical Research Center in Princeton, N.J., Thursday said scientists linked a genetically engineered antibody to an anti-cancer drug called doxorubicin.

- The result: BR96-DOX, a drug that circulates in the bloodstream, finds cancer and "selectively delivers the anti-cancer agent to tumor cells."

FIGURE 1.4
How the text in Figure 1.3 appears when flowed onto the screen in a clustered style.

Chapter 2

Hypertext

Hyper is probably the most important prefix in this book. It refers to the act of linking an object to something that gives to the object a dimension it did not have before it was linked. Simply stated, *hyper* means linked.

Hypertext is text that has been linked. In a hypertext system when you select a line of text by clicking on it with your mouse, your computer displays the object to which that line of text has been linked. The object of the link can be other text, or an image, or a sound, or some video, or any combination thereof.

Linking Text to Other Text

You can link any text to any other text. Consider the example in Figure 2.1. It shows how each bullet in a text slide is linked to another text slide. When you make a presentation with such a hypertext slide, you can instantly switch to any one of the linked

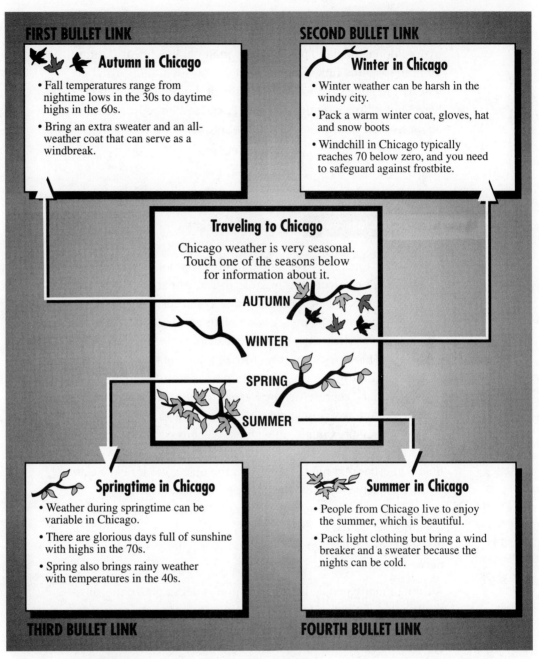

FIGURE 2.1
Hypertext file linked to four other text files.

texts simply by clicking on the bullet that triggers it. This gives you the power to interact with your audience; instead of being forced by traditional media to present your material in a linear fashion, you can instantly link to any part of your presentation. You may fear that making such linkages is difficult, but Part Two of this book shows how easy that is to do. First, read on to learn more about hypertext and the principles of presentation technology.

Hypertext in the Classroom

Hypertext is especially well suited to the classroom because of the way in which curriculum is organized. The course syllabus consists of a list of topics to be covered in class. Each topic has a list of objectives that must be met. Lesson plans are designed to teach each objective. The lesson plans use learning resources to meet the objectives. This curriculum structure of topics, objectives, lessons, and learning resources can be thought of as a multidimensional web that can be represented by hypertext, which teachers can use to have instant access to any topic, objective, lesson plan, or learning resource. For example, the course syllabus could be entered into a text file and flowed onto the screen. To each topic would be linked another text file that contains the objectives for each class. To each objective would be linked the topics and learning resources needed to teach that content. The learning resources need not be limited to text files; they can consist of any multimedia object or application program on the teacher's computer or network.

Although many people believe computers dehumanize the classroom, quite the opposite is true. Nothing is more dehumanizing than teachers who can teach only in the prescribed order in which their materials have been sequenced. When students ask questions, instead of being able to show the audiovisual materials and lecture notes needed to answer, "serial" teachers must tell the students to "...wait until I get there; that slide will be coming up in a few minutes."

In a hyperteaching environment, teachers are more able to interact with students because they can access any lesson plan, any slide, any sound track, and any video clip within a second. Classes become truly interactive when students are able to explore and discover along with their teachers.

Business Applications of Hypertext

In the fast-paced world of business you must be able to access information quickly. Hypertext lets you do just that. You can take any information from any source and organize it any way you want. Because you put it together the way you think of it, it works like you do. If you are meeting with a customer or making a presentation to your boss or board of directors and you need access to some information to prove a point, you can have it on the screen instantly.

Think of the competitive advantage of having such access to all of your product information, pricing, and availability. As you will see in the tutorial in Part Two of this book, if you can use a text editor, you can have this advantage.

Chapter 3

Displaying Pictures

J ust as you can take any text and flow it into a text slide, so also can you display any picture on your computer screen for use during a presentation. The only requirement is that you get the picture into a bitmap format compatible with your presentation software. Your picture can be a slide, transparency, photograph, poster, flat art, or three-dimensional physical object. Described in the sections that follow are techniques for getting various kinds of pictures into a format that can be used with your computer.

35-mm Slides

To get 35-mm slides into your computer, you can either scan or video digitize them. Scanners use light beams that can read thousands of scan lines from your slide. Each scan line is broken down into a series of dots called pixels; *pixel* stands for picture element. The pixels are written to a computer graphics file that produces high-resolution full-color pictures on your computer screen, which consists of a grid of dots that reproduces the pattern of pixels in your picture.

Slide scanners are pricey; a less expensive way of getting 35-mm slides onto your computer screen is to video digitize them. Video digitizers are computer circuit boards that "grab" a frame from an incoming video signal and break it down into a pixel grid that gets written to a computer graphics file. To digitize a 35-mm slide, you can either project it onto a projection screen with a slide projector and then shoot it with a video camera, or you can insert it into a slide-to-video converter, like the one shown in Figure 3.1. Both the camera and the converter produce a video signal that feeds into the digitizing board.

The RasterOps Expresso shown in Figure 3.1 costs about $700. It has a joystick you can use to adjust the red-green-blue content of your slide in case it has faded. Zoom, brightness, and focus controls let you frame and adjust the contrast of your slide. Figure 3.2 shows how you can see the video image on your computer screen while you adjust these controls, making sure the picture appears just the way you want it before you tell your computer to digitize it. This is a real time-saver that makes digitizing slides very efficient.

Flat Art

Figure 3.3 shows a flatbed scanner used to scan flat art such as posters, photographs, and pages out of books. Like the slide scanner previously discussed, the flatbed scanner uses light beams to transfer the artwork into a grid of pixels that is written to a computer graphics file.

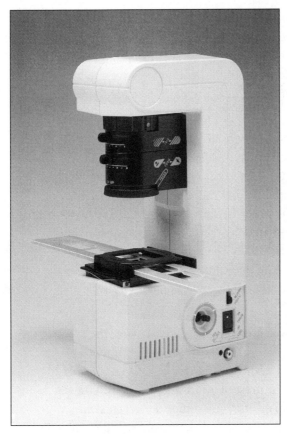

FIGURE 3.1
Framing a slide with a RasterOps
Expresso. Used by permission of
RasterOps.

Flat art can also be digitized by shooting it with a camera
connected to a digitizing board. A time-saving advantage of using a
camera is that you can preview the image; with a scanner you
must wait for the scan to complete before viewing it on your computer screen.

Where portability is important, hand-held scanners are useful, as
demonstrated in Figure 3.4. In fact, hand-held scanning technology has progressed to the point that it rivals the quality of flatbed
scanners. Even though hand-held scanners are only about 4 inches

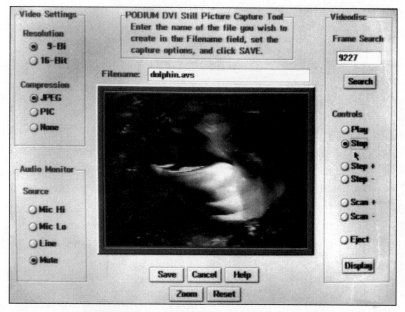

FIGURE 3.2
Previewing a slide before saving it for use in a presentation.
PODIUM screen used by permission of the University of
Delaware.

FIGURE 3.3
A photograph being scanned
on a flatbed scanner. Used by
permission of Hewlett-Packard,
manufacturer of the flatbed
scanner.

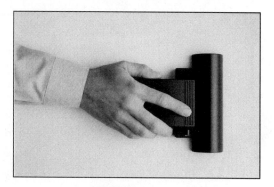

FIGURE 3.4
Materials such as magazine
articles, news clips, and photos
can be scanned by a hand-held
scanner. Used by permission of
Caere Corporation, manufacturer of the hand-held scanner.

wide, they come with software that can be used to "stitch" together larger photos that require multiple passes to be scanned.

Physical Objects

Using photography or video equipment, you can take a picture of any physical object and get it onto your computer screen for use in a presentation. For example, if you have a slide scanner, you can take a 35-mm slide of the object and then scan it into your computer. Shooting 35-mm slides is a wise practice because you can keep the slides for several years; when the computer graphics field progresses to provide better scanners and projectors that can show higher resolution pictures, you will be able to rescan the slides without having to do all your photography again.

If you have a video digitizer, you can get any physical object onto your computer screen by shooting it with your camera and digitizing the resulting video signal. If you can physically bring the object to your computer, you can aim your camera at the object and use a live video feed to digitize it in real time. Otherwise, you can use a camcorder to videotape the object and then replay the tape, connecting the output from your camcorder to the digitizing board. The new generation of Hi8 camcorders has made very high-quality video affordable to the consumer at mass market prices.

Nevertheless, 35-mm slides are still higher in resolution than any camcorder. As previously mentioned, the best way to protect against changes in technology is to shoot 35-mm slides that can be redigitized in the future when graphics formats change.

Clip Art

Clip art libraries are collections of pictures that you can use in presentations. The major computer graphics programs like Corel Systems Corporation's *CorelDraw*, Software Publishing's *Harvard Graphics*, Micrografx's *Graphics Works*, and Lotus's *Freelance* come with clip art libraries containing thousands of pictures. Some clip art fills the screen with complete pictures of objects like jet aircraft, animals, flowers, flags, maps, sports, or famous personalities. Other clip art consists of smaller objects like arrows, button shapes, pointers, or borders that you combine with other pictures to create a composite image.

Bitmaps

The picture you want to use in your presentation may already be a bitmapped computer graphics file. However, due to the lack of standardization in computer graphics image storage formats, the bitmap may not be in a format that your presentation software can use. There are already more than 32 bitmap formats.

Fortunately, utilities can convert bitmaps from one format to another. Some of the more useful programs include Inset Systems' *HiJaak*, JASC's *Paint Shop Pro*, Alchemy Mindworks' *Graphic Workshop*, and Micrografx's *Magic*.

To avoid the extra disk space required to keep images in multiple formats on your computer, it is important to choose a suite of software for use in your school or company that follows a common standard. More is said about this in Chapter 8, which deals with standards.

Hyperpictures

n Chapter 2, which dealt with hypertext, you learned that
you can link any line of any text slide to any other slide on
your computer. Chapter 4 extends this concept to pictures by letting you place invisible triggers any place on any picture. You can
link items to the triggers, just like you can link slides to lines of
hypertext. There is no limit to the number of triggers you can
have on a picture; each trigger can launch a different item that
you link to it. Just as text that is linked is called hypertext, pictures
that contain triggers are called hyperpictures.

Linking Pictures to Text

Consider the example in Figure 4.1. Triggers have been placed on
restaurants on a downtown street. The user can select any restaurant and find out the price range and cuisine served there.

You can extend this concept to any topic for which you can draw a
picture. For example, in making a presentation about jobs avail-

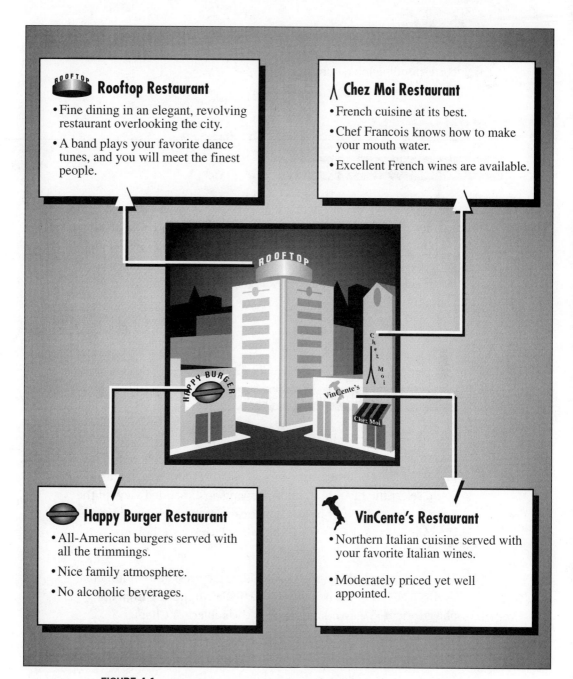

Rooftop Restaurant

- Fine dining in an elegant, revolving restaurant overlooking the city.
- A band plays your favorite dance tunes, and you will meet the finest people.

Chez Moi Restaurant

- French cuisine at its best.
- Chef Francois knows how to make your mouth water.
- Excellent French wines are available.

Happy Burger Restaurant

- All-American burgers served with all the trimmings.
- Nice family atmosphere.
- No alcoholic beverages.

VinCente's Restaurant

- Northern Italian cuisine served with your favorite Italian wines.
- Moderately priced yet well appointed.

FIGURE 4.1
Map of restaurants linked to text slides that describe them.

able in your school or company, you could select different positions in your organizational chart to display information about the corresponding job descriptions.

Linking Pictures to Other Pictures

The triggers on a hyperpicture can also trigger other pictures. For example, in a presentation of human anatomy, you could project a human body and click on body parts to show slides that provide close-ups with more detail. Each of these close-ups could in turn be linked to other pictures providing more detail, which could also contain further links.

Linking Pictures to Any Multimedia Object

Triggers can be linked not only to text slides and other pictures but also to any multimedia event your computer is capable of producing. For example, in the human anatomy presentation, the user could select the heart and, upon viewing an expanded view of the heart, choose different parts of the heart, each of which triggers the sound that a doctor would hear by placing a stethoscope over that location.

This concept of linking triggers to slides, pictures, and multimedia events leads us to think about multimedia computing from an object-oriented viewpoint, which is the subject of Chapter 5.

Object Orientation

rinciple 5 asks you to think of every file on your computer as an object. The objects can consist of text files, images, waveform audio files, digital video, animation sequences, sound tracks, or any application software program installed on your computer or network.

What are these files the objects of? Links. Any object on your computer can be linked to any line of text or any part of any picture in your presentation. The tutorial in Part Two of this book shows how simply you can create links that put you just a mouse click away from showing or playing objects when you want to present them.

Described in the next section is a taxonomy of objects to which you can link hypertext and hyperpicture triggers. Understanding the scope and variety of these linkages will help you take maximum advantage of the capabilities of object-oriented presentation technology.

Picture objects include slides, illustrations, clip art, and photographs. Because any picture can be drawn or digitized onto your computer screen, any visual can be the object of a link. Hyperpictures can also be the objects of links; that is, the pictures can contain invisible triggers that are in turn linked to other objects.

In an effective presentation system there is no limit to the amount of linking you can have. Any object can be linked to any object or combination of objects any number of times. The tutorial in Part Two of this book shows how you can take advantage of this infinite capability to link.

Slide Banks

Instead of being forced to show slides in a predetermined order dictated by a carousel slide tray, you can have multiple links to your slides that allow you to show exactly the slide you want when you want it. You can have instant access to thousands of slides, and you can show any one of them within a second.

Product Illustrations

Think of how effective your marketing reps can be while talking with customers about their products. Instead of being limited to the number of slides that fit in a carousel tray, you can have slides of all your products and use hypertext links to organize them according to product lines. If a customer is not interested in what you are showing and says, "If only you could show me this product in a more affordable version," you would be able to have it on the screen instantly. Then you would be just a mouse click away from the pricing and ordering procedures needed to make the sale.

Clip Art

When you do not have the time or money to develop custom graphics, you can turn to clip art libraries. They contain objects of interest to businessmen as well as educators. For example, the clip art library that comes with *Micrografx Draw!* has the picture of

FIGURE 5.1
Clip art from the *Micrografx Draw!* library.

Abraham Lincoln in Figure 5.1; the *Harvard Graphics* clip art library contains the map of the Mideast in Figure 5.2; and the *CorelDraw* clip art library contains the commanding officer's insignia in Figure 5.3.

Photographs

Using the scanning and digitizing technology previously described, any photograph can become the object of a link. It can be a black and white or a full-color display. Like slides, you can have instant access to any photographic image on your computer.

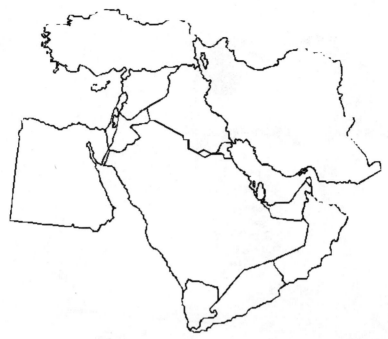

FIGURE 5.2
Clip art from the *Harvard Graphics* library.

FIGURE 5.3
Clip art from the *CorelDraw* library.

It is amazing how much an audio sound track can do for a slide. Audio can make it seem like still images have come to life, even though they do not move. A technique called *ambient sound* has you record the sounds associated with an object and play them back when you show the still image. Even though the picture does not move, the ambient sound creates an atmosphere suggesting that the object is in motion.

The National Geographic Society's Whales videodisc makes excellent use of sound under stills to demonstrate the feeding habits of humpback whales. The three slides pictured in Figures 5.4, 5.5,

FIGURE 5.4
Humpback whale blowing a ring of bubbles to form bubble net. Photo used by permission of the National Geographic Society.

FIGURE 5.5
Humpback whale is below water
surface preparing to swim up
through the finished ring of bubbles. Photo used by permission of
the National Geographic Society.

and 5.6 show how the humpback blows a ring of bubbles called a
bubble net to trap small fish and then swims up through the ring
to eat. These three still images are accompanied by the sounds the
whale makes as it blows the ring of bubbles. Even though the pictures do not move, the ambient sound creates the illusion of
movement.

Instructional Commentary

Using a waveform audio digitizer board and a microphone, you
can record instructional commentary and link it to a slide. When
the slide appears in your presentation, it triggers the audio, and
your audience hears the commentary you recorded.

An effective technique is to include ambient sound in the background when you record the commentary. Not only will the audience hear the commentary, but also they will be affected by the
ambient sound that adds realism and conjures up the illusion of
motion in the picture.

Commercial Sound Bites

Marketing reps can digitize the sound tracks from their commer-
cials and link them to the appropriate images in a presentation. It

FIGURE 5.6
Humpback whale surfacing with a
tasty mouthful. Photo used by permission of the National Geographic
Society.

is also possible to have the first image in a sequence of slides trigger
an audio track and then have subsequent images appear in synchronization with the sound bite. The tutorial in Part Two shows
you how to do that.

Music
You can link music from a variety of sources. If the music is on a
compact disc and your computer has a CD-ROM drive, you can
make clips on the CD the objects of your links; otherwise, you can
record the music from the CD onto your hard disk drive with an
audio digitizer and link the resulting audio files to your presentation.

If your computer has a Musical Instrumental Digital Interface
(MIDI), you may want to consider using MIDI to provide background music. MIDI is the most economical way to add music to
your presentations because instead of recording all of the waveform information like a digital audio board, it records only the
performance gestures (such as note on, note off, louder, softer)
needed for a synthesizer to play the music.

Low-cost, compact MIDI synthesizers are now available that connect either to a MIDI board inside your computer or to your computer's serial port. The sound is incredibly impressive; recent

breakthroughs in digital sound synthesis have propelled these little MIDI boxes to symphonic proportions. For more portability you can also get sound cards that have synthesizer chips on board, alleviating the need for external music boxes.

Video

Just as you can link any text, any picture, and any sound, so also can any video be the object of a link. There are three technologies for storing and accessing video during your presentation: videotape, videodisc, and digital video.

Computer-controlled Videotape

Computer-controlled VCRs can be used to play clips from videotapes during your presentations. However, videotapes have the extreme limitation of slow access times. On a 2-hour videotape it can take as long as 3 minutes to find the starting location of the clip you want to show.

It is better to use videotape only to show video in which the clips are shown sequentially; you put them on the tape in the order you plan to show them, thereby avoiding slow access times.

For truly interactive video, you need a medium that can quickly search frames; videodisc and digital video can do that.

Interactive Videodisc

Thousands of videodiscs have already been pressed for use in education and training; they are cataloged in *The Videodisc Compendium* (1993). Videodiscs are popular because they provide very fast access to any frame of video. In addition to storing motion sequences, videodiscs also have a stereo sound track; the two tracks can be played together to create a true stereo effect, or they can hold different audio. For example, one track might contain an English narration while the other carries a Spanish translation. Or one track might contain an advanced narration with more basic explanations on the other.

Eiser (1992) tells how videodiscs have proven so effective in education that the states of California and Texas have adopted videodiscs in place of textbooks, investing former textbook budgets in videodisc technology instead. Videodiscs also enjoy widespread adoption in military and industrial training, and many prospective new-car buyers have used videodiscs to learn about all the various options and selling points of the automobile they are being sold.

Videodiscs have one obvious disadvantage: because videodisc is a read-only medium, you cannot write your own unless you have a costly videodisc mastering machine. However, for as little as $300, you can send a videotape to a videodisc production house and have a videodisc pressed, and if you pay for overnight postage, you can even get next-day service. If you need large quantities of your videodisc, you can have a master disc made for about $2,000 per side, which can be used to press copies costing from $10 to $20, depending upon the quantity. Videodisc production houses are listed in Part Three of this book.

Digital Video Recording and Playback
For users who want to record and play back their own video, digital video has arrived. If you have a digital video capture board in your computer, you can use digital video software to record from any video source, and then you can have instant access to it during your presentations. For example, you could record a live video feed from a camera, or a videotape or disc, or a television broadcast.

Live Video Feeds
If you have a digital video capture board, you can even link direct video feeds to your presentation items. For example, suppose an important event is happening in the news, and you have a cable TV feed connected to your digital video capture board; your presentation software can put you just a mouse click away from having that video on your screen when you need it during your presentation.

Documentaries
Of the many applications of interactive video, one of the most important is to document current events. Some of the more

famous examples are the John F. Kennedy assassination, the collapse of the Berlin Wall, and the Rodney King beating. By incorporating such videos into your presentation, you can make the classroom or boardroom come alive.

Recruiting

Interactive video is a powerful recruiting tool. By including clips that advertise the strong points of your institution or business, and front-ending them with a hyperpicture menu that lets clients browse at will, you can recruit students to colleges and universities, attract high school seniors to military service, woo potential clients, and encourage the brightest college graduates to apply to your business or graduate school.

Animations

Animations are like video in that they contain motion, but instead of shooting video of real objects in motion, animation sequences use computers to generate and animate objects digitally. Many presentation tools have animation capability. *Storyboard* and *Tool-Book* have recorders that let you move an object around the screen while the computer keeps a record of the points to which you moved it; then you can play back the sequence of movements to create an animation of the object.

More sophisticated animation software like *AutoDesk Animator* and *3D Studio* lets you specify functions that control the movement of objects dynamically. For example, you can draw an object, set a target or path, and specify that you want the object to move to the target in a specified number of seconds; the animation software makes it happen.

Animations can be the objects of links in your presentations; some applications of animations are discussed in the following sections.

Physics, Mechanics, Chemistry, and Anatomy

Animation software can help students visualize difficult concepts. For example, with Andomeda Software's *GRAVITY for Windows* you can set the mass and velocity vectors of planets and see their effects on planetary movement. With the University of Minnesota's *Lincages* you can synthesize mechanisms and watch animations that put cams and gears through their full range of motion.

In Falcon Software's *Introduction to General Chemistry* animations show acid-base reactions, how to measure pH, and atmospheric pressure. Lea and Febiger's *Dynamics of Human Anatomy* contains animations that show blood flow through the heart, capillary exchange, valve action in venous return, and isotonic muscle contraction. Particularly impressive is the excitation of a skeletal muscle fiber at a neuromuscular junction.

Product Illustrations

Animations can help your marketing reps present products. By showing an animation of how your product works, you can differentiate it from the competition's, helping the customer understand why yours is better.

Maintenance Procedures

Animations can also be used to show technicians how to make repairs. By viewing the animation while making the repair, the technician can complete it more quickly and with less chance of omitting an essential step or making some other mistake.

Software

In an object-oriented presentation system, you can also link other software applications that reside on your computer or network. When you select a presentation item that is linked to another software application, your computer launches the other program;

when you complete it, you return to the point in your presentation at which you triggered the launch.

An important advantage of this capability is that you can make it easy for employees to work with software they might otherwise have difficulty running and keeping track of. Instead of having to learn how to work an operating system and remember what is running where, the presentation package can handle all of these management tasks, letting the user simply select presentation items that trigger other applications.

Tutorials, Drills, and Tests

The computer-assisted instruction movement of the past quarter century has produced thousands of tutorials, drills, and tests that can be the objects of links in your presentation. You can also use an authoring system such as *Authorware, Quest, ToolBook,* or *Ten-CORE* to create lessons and link them to presentation items.

Suppose you use the hyperpicture capability to create a kiosk application. The user comes to your kiosk and starts browsing. At a certain point you want to collect some information from the user, so you put in a link to a survey produced with a testing package such as *The Examiner.*

Demography and Statistics

QUE's *DemoGraphics* software contains a database of the most important demographic parameters for nearly every country in the world. You can link this package to your presentation and use it to demonstrate the effect of birth rates, life expectancy, fertility, and mortality on world populations. You set the variables and your computer graphs the results, projecting ahead for the number of years you specify. Birth and death rates can be adjusted to reflect changing demographic conditions like famine and war.

You can use the *Systat* exploratory data analysis software to let customers or students play "what if" games by changing the values of variables that affect outcomes. For example, you can change the value of the *y-coordinate* of data points and watch how that changes the regression line. Fridlund (1993) tells how you can use this to "...regress acoustic decay against an exponential model, or regress judgment data to a power function." Forecasters can detrend and seasonally decompose their time series, or make forecasts using either exponential smoothing or a full Box-Jenkins auto-regressive integrated moving average. *Systat*'s traveling salesman routine finds the shortest path connecting locations on a map or points on a scatterplot.

Spreadsheet Graphs of Corporate Data

You can link presentation items to spreadsheet graphs of corporate data and have all of your organization's information available at the click of the mouse. The tutorial in Part Two shows you how to make links that are dynamic; that is, instead of showing a slide that you prepared in advance, your presentation launches the spreadsheet software and makes it graph the current state of your data. Any last-minute changes in the data are reflected in the resulting chart or graph.

Just-in-Time Training

Object-oriented systems can save time and money. Suppose you are a technician who encounters difficulty trying to repair a complex machine. A hypertext repair manual puts you just a few mouse clicks away from the training you need, complete with full-motion video that shows how to make the repair.

Chapter 6

Hypermedia

So far this book has introduced two terms that use the prefix *hyper*: *hypertext*, which refers to text that has been linked, and *hyperpicture*, which refers to a picture containing one or more triggers that have been linked. Principle 6 uses the prefix *hyper* in a more general way by combining it with the word *media* to create the term *hypermedia*.

Linking Media to Form Hypermedia

Text and pictures are two forms of media. Other media include audio, video, animation sequences, and any application on your computer or network that produces output you can see or hear. Any of these media can be the object of a link, hence the more general term *hypermedia*, which refers to media that are linked.

Hypertext and Hyperpictures

In addition to linking hypertext and hyperpictures to other text and pictures, you can also link them to any object on your computer. This means that while making a presentation, you not only have instant access to all of your text files, but also you can access instantly any one of thousands of slides, audio clips, motion sequences, animations, and any application program on your computer or network.

For example, if you link a sound bite to a slide, the slide triggers the sound bite when you show it. If you have a series of slides with timed waits in between them, they appear in synchronization with the sound track, which could be explaining the pictures.

Hyperaudio and Hypervideo

In addition to putting links in text files, you can put links in pictures, and you can use audio and video clips to trigger other multimedia events. When audio is used to trigger events, it is called hyperaudio; similarly, when a video cue triggers another event, it is called hypervideo.

Chapter 7

Metaphors

Metaphors help you understand something new by thinking about it in terms of something with which you are already familiar. The following metaphors are particularly helpful in understanding multimedia presentation technology.

Virtual Slide Tray

Most presentation graphics programs use a slide tray metaphor whereby you think of your images as slides that can be placed anywhere in a tray. You insert the slides in the order in which you plan to show them, and the software lets you use your mouse to click through them, just like the hand control on a slide projector.

As Canning (1992) noted in his review, most commercial presentation packages never get past this elementary form of slide show that limits the presenter to one tray of slides that must be shown sequentially even though there are no physical reasons why presentation software should limit you to a single tray like a slide projector does. You can accomplish so much more if your presentation software lets you work with multiple slide trays. Instead of being forced to use just one tray, you should be able to access any number of trays, any time you want. Each tray can contain an infinite number of slides, and you can put any slide in any tray any number of times.

You organize your slides into as many trays as you like, linking the trays to your presentation items. Then when you are giving your presentation, you can instantly access any tray by choosing the item to which it is linked. This lets you become a creative speaker who can sense the needs of the moment and show just the right materials. You will be most effective when students or customers ask questions because you can instantly link to items that help you answer them.

Virtual Multimedia Carousel Tray

Normally you think of a carousel tray holding slides, which is what it was designed to do. However, on a multimedia computer you can think of the slots in the virtual tray as being able to hold much more than static slides. For example, one slot could hold a video clip that knows where to start and stop when you show it. Another slot could hold a sound track that explains the content of a slide. Still another slot might hold an animation sequence. The same virtual capability you have to show slides extends to the entire field of multimedia when you consider these advantages of a multimedia carousel tray.

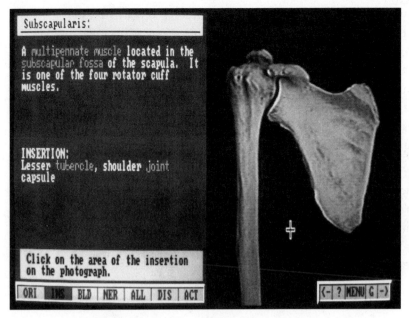

FIGURE 7.1
Mask overlays left half of a videodisc image from Lea and
Febiger's Dynamics of Human Anatomy videodisc. Used by
permission of Lea and Febiger.

Overlay and Underlay

Slides can overlay video to provide a mask that hides unwanted
information or highlights areas of emphasis. Lea and Febiger's gold
medal–winning *Exploring Human Anatomy* uses this technique
effectively. For example, Figure 7.1 shows how an overlay masks
the left half of a videodisc image, revealing on the right a human
shoulder bone. In Figure 7.2, a bitmap of the subscapularis muscle
overlays the shoulder bone to show the location of this rotator cuff
muscle. Figure 7.3 shows another bitmap overlay that identifies
the blood vessels and nerves that feed and control this muscle.

Figure 7.4 illustrates how slides and video can underlay the text of
your bullets, providing an effective backdrop capability. You learn
how to make backdrops in Part Two of this book.

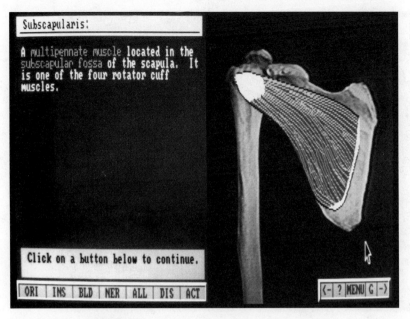

FIGURE 7.2
Bitmap overlays shoulder bone to locate the subscapularis muscle in Lea and Febiger's Dynamics of Human Anatomy videodisc. Used by permission of Lea and Febiger.

Cinematic Effects

Multimedia presentation software provides a rich variety of cinematic special effects that can enhance your presentation. Just like special effects are used in movies to create excitement and enhance the film, so also can they be used to add pizzazz to your presentation. Each object in your presentation can have special effects associated with it.

For example, slides can be "wiped out" or "dissolved" on the screen, timed to take longer or appear very quickly depending on the need, and made to advance automatically to the next item in your virtual multimedia tray. Sound tracks can be played loud or soft, and they can be made to start and stop at any location you choose. Video can be sized to fill the screen or cut to fill a window in your slide.

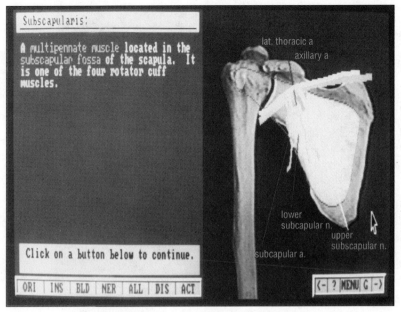

FIGURE 7.3
Bitmap overlays to identify blood vessels and nerves in Lea
and Febiger's Dynamics of Human Anatomy videodisc.
Used by permission of Lea and Febiger.

Navigating Hyperspace

When you use multimedia presentation software that is object-
oriented, you become a navigator, able to move anywhere in your
presentation quickly and easily. The connections you make by
linking slides, bullets, audio, and video can be thought of as a web
through which you navigate. Because you create the web when
you outline your presentation, you can navigate it quickly and
naturally to show the items you need precisely when you want
them. Nevermore will you have to tell a student or customer who
has asked a question, "Sorry, you will have to wait; I will answer
your question when we come to that slide."

FIGURE 7.4
Picture underlaying presentation bullets—a simple yet effective technique.

Digital Chalk

Multimedia presentation software should give you the capability to draw on your computer screen, to add information to your slide, or to underline or point things out. It is as if you were using a piece of chalk on a blackboard, except that on the computer you can draw on top of anything—even motion video while it is playing back.

If you want to draw in finer detail than you can with a mouse, mouse pens let you draw with a stylus and still have the other functions of a mouse available. For example, Figure 7.5 shows a presenter using an Imsi *PC Stylus* mouse pen to annotate a slide.

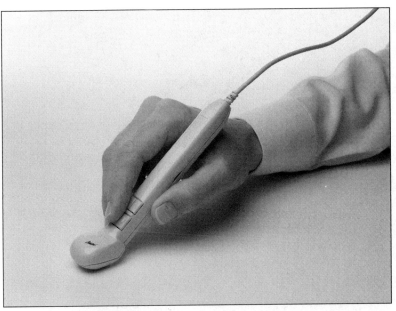

FIGURE 7.5
Using a mouse pen to write with digital chalk on slide. Used by permission of Imsi, manufacturer of the mouse pen.

Multimedia Portfolio

The most frustrating aspect of traditional media is that all the work you do preparing for a presentation gets undone afterward when you have to remove the slides from your tray either to put them in some different order for another talk or to return them to the slide library from which you borrowed them. With multimedia presentation technology there is no need to undo anything. As you will see in Part Two of this book, the content of a virtual slide tray is defined by a simple list that you type into your computer. These lists are standard text files that occupy very little space on your computer. Instead of deleting the file after your presentation, you keep it on your system so it will be ready the next time you want it. Because you never have to undo anything, you gradually build a repertoire of multimedia lesson plans, presentation outlines, and virtual carousel trays.

Hyperlecturing

Text that is linked is called hypertext. Pictures that are linked are called hyperpictures. In a like manner, lecturers who are linked can be referred to as hyperlecturers. The hyperlecturer is the most powerful presenter of all. Instead of being molded by traditional media that force you to follow a predetermined sequence of events, the hyperlecturer can link to any slide, text, graphic, audio, or video clip within a second.

Chapter 8

Standards

The multimedia computer industry is beset by an unfortunate lack of standardization. Instead of uniting the nation's best minds to create a compatible cross-platform system for delivering multimedia instruction, the computer industry is hard at work creating multiple standards and competing products. If this were happening accidentally, one might be more willing to tolerate the situation. Instead, vendors intentionally create disparity to differentiate their products from the competition and to obsolete past purchases so customers will buy more hardware. In the area of graphics alone, there are now more than 30 so-called "standards" for storing pictures in computer files. If an industry provides 30 different ways of doing something, there is no standard.*

Computer industry leaders fail to recognize how self-defeating this lack of standardization is. They should learn a lesson from the musicians. During the early 1980s, the National Association of

---

*The first six paragraphs of Chapter 8 are based on a guest editorial written by the author in T.H.E. Journal (Hofstetter, 1993).

Music Merchants and the Audio Engineering Society began to discuss how the lack of standards was retarding the market for music synthesizers. Consumers were afraid to buy a keyboard because there was no guarantee that it would be compatible with later models in the same product line, much less with synthesizers made by other vendors. In 1983, the MIDI standard was released, and all of the music merchants endorsed it. Consumers were no longer afraid of obsolescence, and music synthesizer sales mushroomed. Vendors made more money not so much because their market share increased but rather because through standardization the entire market grew exponentially.

Instead of having one multimedia standard, presenters are faced with a complicated array of competing software and hardware platforms that can be described as "multi-multimedia." When you create a presentation, you must be careful to store your objects in formats that will have the most longevity and compatibility. Otherwise the time and effort you spend will have to be reinvested when the so-called standards change.

Media Control Interface (MCI)

Microsoft's Media Control Interface (MCI) may provide a strategic approach to coping with this lack of standardization. The purpose of the MCI is to provide a device-independent means of developing multimedia software. The idea is that vendors who make multimedia hardware supply for each multimedia device an MCI translation table. Instead of hard-coding applications to specific devices, developers use MCI commands that get converted automatically by the translation table into the specific instructions needed to control the device. The MCI commands consist of generic multimedia instructions like PLAY, RECORD, PAUSE, SEEK, SAVE, and STOP.

For example, consider the industry-wide problem posed by the differences among videodisc players. Not only do videodisc command sets vary between vendors, but even within a product line manufacturers change the commands on different models. When developers want to show a videodisc frame number, they must write the code needed to display it on all the different brands. If MCI were adopted as an industry-wide standard, instead of hard-coding the commands needed to display the videodisc frame on every specific player, the application would simply send the MCI command SEEK TO the frame number. If every videodisc manufacturer provided a device driver with an MCI translation table, then the user could attach any videodisc player, just like MIDI lets musicians use any keyboard.

If the Microsoft MCI were adopted as an industry-wide standard, it would significantly reduce the amount of time lost due to the lack of standardization. However, other vendors are developing different standards. Until the vendors unite behind a common strategy, the multitude of multimedia will increase, making multimedia more "multi" in the wrong sense of the word. While multimedia has the potential to improve education and communication tremendously, multi-multimedia retards its development and hinders its widespread adoption.

Videodisc Slides and Motion Sequences

The MCI addresses videodiscs by frame numbers. There are two industry-wide formats for videodiscs: CAV and CLV. CAV discs can store up to 54,000 still frames or 30 minutes of motion video with a stereo sound track. The frames are addressed simply by specifying numbers from 1 to 54,000. The CAV format lets you display still frames as well as play motion sequences.

CLV discs can store up to an hour of video on each disc side, which is twice as much video as CAV discs hold. However, unless you have an expensive high-end player such as the Pioneer LD-V8000, you cannot show still frames from CLV discs. The MCI addresses

CLV discs by minute and second. For example, the address 16:24 would make your computer start playing 16 minutes and 24 seconds from the start of the disc.

Because the capability to show still frames is so important in presentation graphics, the CAV format is better for presentations. However, if you need to access more than 30 minutes of video at one time, you need either the CLV format or the more forward-looking digital video format discussed in the next section.

Digital Video Interactive (DVI)

At Fall COMDEX 1992, IBM and Intel won "Best of Show" with their Digital Video Interactive (DVI) product called ActionMedia II. Available both for the Micro Channel and the industry standard AT bus, the ActionMedia board lets you digitize still images, audio, and full-motion video direct to your hard disk drive and then have frame-addressable access when you play it back. The video plays back full screen at 30 frames per second with a quality approaching that of television.

When Microsoft announced plans to develop *Video for Windows*, Intel negotiated to have the DVI file format included as one of its options. As a result, the IBM/Intel ActionMedia II board is now supported under the MCI as one of the options for recording and playing back *Video for Windows* files.

While it is possible to play back *Video for Windows* files without a digital video board, when this book went to press the quality of unassisted playback was not very good; images appear pixellated and jerky. However, much research is being conducted to discover more efficient digital video encoding and playback algorithms, and the quality of unassisted digital video playback will certainly improve.

Video Overlay

If your computer has a video overlay board, you can display videotapes and videodisc images on the same screen as your computer graphics. As you will see in the tutorial part of this book, you can even overlay text and graphics on video images.

There are many video overlay boards on the market. You must be careful to choose a board supported by all the software you want to use it with. Sometimes you encounter impossible situations in which one application requires a circuit board that goes in the same slot as another circuit board required by another application.

Microsoft's MCI provides a standard for video overlay. Any video overlay card for which there is an MCI device driver works with any software that also uses the MCI. Because the MCI only works with Windows, DOS users who do not have Windows cannot take advantage of it. Having the MCI is a very good reason to move to Windows.

Compact Disc "Red Book" Audio

Thanks to the audio recording industry, there is an international standard for addressing music on compact discs called red book addressing. A red book address has three numbers that can specify the minute, second, and frame of any audio on a CD. For example, the red book address 21:46:53 specifies the frame of audio at 21 minutes, 46 seconds, and 53 frames into the CD. Compact discs have 75 frames per second.

DOS, Windows, and OS/2 users can all use red book addressing because there are red book drivers for all three operating systems. When you purchase a CD-ROM drive, make sure the vendor supplies a driver for the operating system you use.

Waveform Audio

There are more than a dozen formats for recording and storing waveform audio files, and many vendors market digital audio boards that compete for the waveform audio market. The Microsoft MCI provides a standard for waveform audio that makes all of these boards work basically the same with software that supports the MCI. Once again, waveform audio provides a good reason for using Windows, if you have not already begun to use it.

MIDI Audio

MIDI may be the most *standard* standard. No matter what MIDI synthesizer, MIDI card, or operating system you have, a MIDI file can be made to play back on your computer.

Problems can arise if you have an early synthesizer that does not follow the "General MIDI" specification that standardizes patches. If someone gives you a MIDI file and the patches on your synthesizer do not match the ones used to record the file, it may play back with the wrong instruments. Once again, the Microsoft MCI comes to the rescue by providing a MIDI mapper that redirects the patches in the MIDI file to match those on your synthesizer.

Bitmapped Graphics

Unfortunately, the Microsoft MCI does not deal with bitmapped graphics. This is perhaps the area where help is most desperately needed because there are so many graphics standards.

To discuss the pluses and minuses of all the different standards is beyond the scope of this book; however, the following advice is offered. If you are a DOS user, store your graphics in the PCX file format. Windows and OS/2 users should use the BMP format. Practically every DOS program that uses graphics can deal with PCX files, and likewise, almost every Windows and OS/2 program works with BMP files.

OS/2 users should beware that the BMP format used by OS/2 is not the same as the one used by Windows. Not all OS/2 programs can read Windows bitmaps, and many Windows programs do not read OS/2 bitmaps. The tutorial in Part Two uses software in which Windows bitmaps can be read under OS/2. Part Three of this book tells how to change formats if you have a bitmap that you want to use with a program that cannot read it.

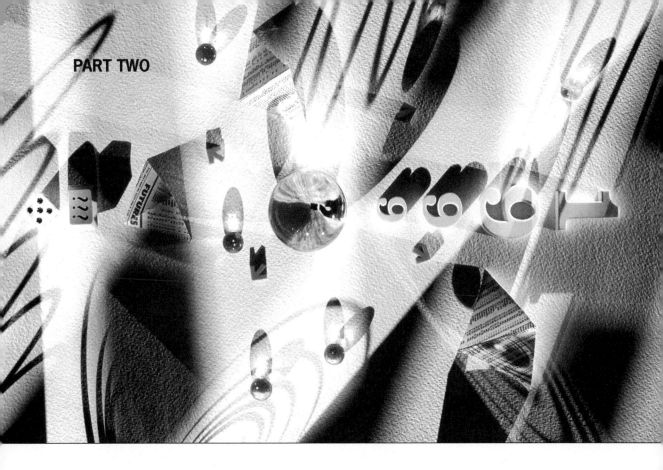

PART TWO

Primer

Now that you have learned the basics of presentation technology, it is time to put them into practice with a tutorial that shows how to create a presentation. As explained in the introduction to this book, you have two options. Either you can read through the tutorial to find out what it would be like to create a presentation, or you can use the PODIUM software that came with this book to work through the exercises and actually create a live presentation.

Chapter 9

An Introduction to PODIUM Presentation Software

PODIUM is multimedia presentation software that lets anyone who can use a text editor or word processor become a master of multimedia. Following the basic principles explained in Part One of this book, PODIUM lets you flow any text onto the screen, and by means of a single keystroke, link any object on your computer to any line of the text. Likewise, PODIUM lets you display any picture on the screen and link any object to any part of that picture. The word processor interface makes PODIUM so easy to use that you can prepare custom presentations the night before, or even the morning of, a lecture.

Although PODIUM was inspired by a desire to improve the quality of lecture presentations (hence its name), it can also be used by individuals to explore large databases of digitized slides, compact disc audio, digital video, and videodisc slides and motion sequences. Teachers can use any word processor to organize the material, and students can use PODIUM to explore it. PODIUM can run either on a personal computer or on a Local Area Network (LAN). By keeping your multimedia objects on a network file server, you can provide access for any user in your organization. When you want to make changes to your presentations, you change only the network copy.

PODIUM also has a "digital chalk" feature that lets you write on any text slide, still image, or motion sequence. When you press and hold down both mouse buttons at the same time, the mouse cursor becomes a piece of chalk. With digital chalk you can write down ideas or emphasize existing points directly on-screen during your presentations.

PODIUM comes in three versions: DOS, Windows, and OS/2 Presentation Manager. The core of PODIUM runs exactly the same way in all three versions. All three require that your computer have VGA graphics. All three work the same with respect to hypertext, hyperbullets, hyperpictures, videodisc slides, motion sequences, and compact disc audio clips. Memory requirements, multimedia options, and other differences among the three versions are described in the sections that follow. While optional adapter cards are mentioned, none are needed for the tutorial in this book.

PODIUM for DOS

PODIUM for DOS requires 2 megabytes of RAM. One megabyte is used as working space by PODIUM, and the second megabyte is used to buffer images that must be stored in either PCX or AVC format. PODIUM keeps three images in this buffer: the one you are viewing, the one you displayed last, and the next one that will appear when you click your mouse. By buffering images, PODIUM responds instantly to your mouse clicks as you move back and forth in a set of slides.

Video overlay can be accomplished via the IBM M-Motion Video Adapter on Micro Channel machines or the CompuVid School Board on the industry standard AT bus. PODIUM for DOS lets you connect up to three video inputs and switch among them during your presentation. For example, you could have a videodisc on input one, a videotape on input two, and a live video feed on input three.

The primary advantage of PODIUM for DOS is that it runs on low-cost PCs and is easy for DOS users who either cannot afford or prefer not to use Windows.

PODIUM for Windows

Windows users will definitely prefer PODIUM for Windows; its menu bar and windowed user interface make it very easy to use. PODIUM for Windows requires 4 megabytes of RAM and Windows 3.1 or higher; bitmaps must be stored in the Windows BMP format.

PODIUM for Windows supports the Microsoft MCI, and it will work with any audio or video adapter for which there is a Windows MCI driver. PODIUM supports the full range of Windows multimedia devices, including waveform digital audio, compact disc audio, videodisc, video overlay, digital video, animation sequences, *Video for Windows*, and MIDI.

PODIUM for Presentation Manager

OS/2 users will prefer PODIUM for Presentation Manager. It requires 6 megabytes of RAM and OS/2 version 2.0 or higher. Bitmaps may be stored in either Windows or OS/2 BMP format.

PODIUM for Presentation Manager supports the Intel/IBM DVI standard and includes tools for digitizing still images, waveform digital audio, and full-motion video using the DVI ActionMedia II Adapter, which is available for the Micro Channel as well as the industry standard AT bus. All Pioneer and SONY videodisc players with serial computer interfaces are supported, with or without the ActionMedia II adapter.

Like PODIUM for Windows, PODIUM for Presentation Manager has a menu bar and windowed user interface that make it very easy to use.

Chapter 10

Using the PODIUM CD-ROM

T he CD-ROM that came with this book contains demonstration and tutorial versions of PODIUM for DOS, PODIUM for Windows, and PODIUM for Presentation Manager. They are identical to the retail versions except that they let you run the demonstration and the tutorial only. If you decide that you like the PODIUM approach and you want to use it for other presentations, you can use the discount coupon in Appendix A to purchase a retail copy.

You may freely copy the contents of the CD-ROM onto the hard disk drive of any computer on which you would like to try the tutorial. If you do not have a CD-ROM player, find a friend, a public library, a school, or a business associate who does, and use it to copy the PODIUM files onto your own diskettes from which you can install the software on your computer. Step-by-step instructions for doing this are provided in Appendix B.

If you already own a retail copy of PODIUM, you can use it instead of installing the tutorial that comes with this book. However, there are a few bitmaps on the CD-ROM that you will need. Assuming your CD-ROM is drive D and your hard drive is C, here are the commands to type to copy those bitmaps:

DOS users:	copy d:\podium*.pcx c:\podium
Windows users:	copy d:\wnpodium*.bmp c:\wnpodium
OS/2 users:	copy d:\pmpodium*.bmp c:\pmpodium

If your computer has a CD-ROM drive, you can install PODIUM directly from that drive. Simply insert the disc that came with this book into your CD-ROM drive, and follow the setup instructions appropriate to your system.

PODIUM for DOS Setup

In the root directory of the CD-ROM is a program titled SETUPDOS; to install PODIUM, run the SETUPDOS program. For example, suppose your CD-ROM is drive D. Here is what you would type:

```
d:\setupdos
```

PODIUM asks you for the name of the drive on which to install itself; respond with the letter name of your hard disk drive, which is probably C. PODIUM then installs itself in a directory called PODIUM on that drive. To run PODIUM, execute the PODEMO.EXE program in your PODIUM directory. For example, if you installed PODIUM on drive C, you would type the following:

```
c:\
cd podium
podemo
```

PODIUM for DOS requires that you have a mouse driver installed on your computer plus the Microsoft extended memory driver HIMEM.SYS. If you are using *SideKick* with PODIUM, make sure your CONFIG.SYS file contains values at least this large for the following parameters:

    files=30
    buffers=30

PODIUM for Windows Setup

From your Windows Program Manager, pull down the Files menu and choose Run; a dialog box appears with a command line field. In the command line, enter the letter name of your CD-ROM drive, followed by SETUPWIN.EXE, and then press ENTER. For example, if your CD-ROM is drive D, you would type the following command line:

    d:\setupwin.exe

PODIUM asks you for the name of the drive on which to install itself; respond with the letter name of your hard disk drive, which is probably C. PODIUM then installs itself in a directory called WNPODIUM on that drive. To run PODIUM, double-click on the PODIUM icon you will find on your Windows desktop.

PODIUM for Presentation Manager Setup

At an OS/2 full-screen prompt, enter the letter name of your CD-ROM drive, followed by SETUPOS2, and then press ENTER. For example, if your CD-ROM is drive D, you would type the following:

    d:\setupos2

PODIUM asks you for the name of the drive on which to install itself; respond with the letter name of your hard disk drive, which is probably C. PODIUM then installs itself in a directory called PMPODIUM on that drive. To run PODIUM, double-click on the PODIUM icon you will find on your OS/2 desktop.

Chapter 11

Beginning the Tutorial– Total Quality Management

Total Quality Management (TQM) is a process that many companies are using to improve operations and increase productivity. Schools are also beginning to realize the benefits of the TQM process. This tutorial shows you how to build a presentation that explains the TQM process. The tutorial guides you through the steps involved in making a presentation. These steps include planning the presentation and creating the home presentation file, linking it to other presentation files and multimedia objects, and adding special effects. The infinite links you can create and the special effects you can add are tools that enhance your presentation and may even help you persuade your audience.

Running the PODIUM Demonstration

PODIUM starts with a demonstration that always appears unless you run some other presentation. Try the demonstration to become familiar with using a mouse to control a PODIUM presentation. The PODIUM title screen is shown in Figure 11.1. DOS users will see it as a full screen; Windows and OS/2 users will see it in a window. To make it fill the screen, Windows and OS/2 users can press the F2 function key. F2 is a toggle; each time you press it, F2 makes PODIUM fill the screen or go back into a window.

Click anywhere on the title screen with your left mouse button to make PODIUM show the demonstration menu. From now on, any time this tutorial tells you to click on something without saying which button to press, you should always press the left mouse button. Now click on "What PODIUM Does," and a text slide appears describing the goal of PODIUM. Click anywhere on that slide to return to the demonstration menu.

Click on "Digitized Slides and Pictures." When the first slide appears, click on it with your left mouse button to see the second slide. On the second slide, press your right mouse button. See how the first slide appears again? When you are showing slides with PODIUM, the mouse works just like a 35-mm slide control; pressing the left button moves forward to the next slide in the tray, and pressing the right button moves back to the previous slide. When you press your left mouse button on the last slide in a tray, PODIUM returns you to the menu.

Spend some time exploring the other items in the PODIUM demonstration. When you are ready to quit PODIUM, DOS users should press F2 and click on Quit. Windows and OS/2 users can pull down the Navigate menu and choose Quit.

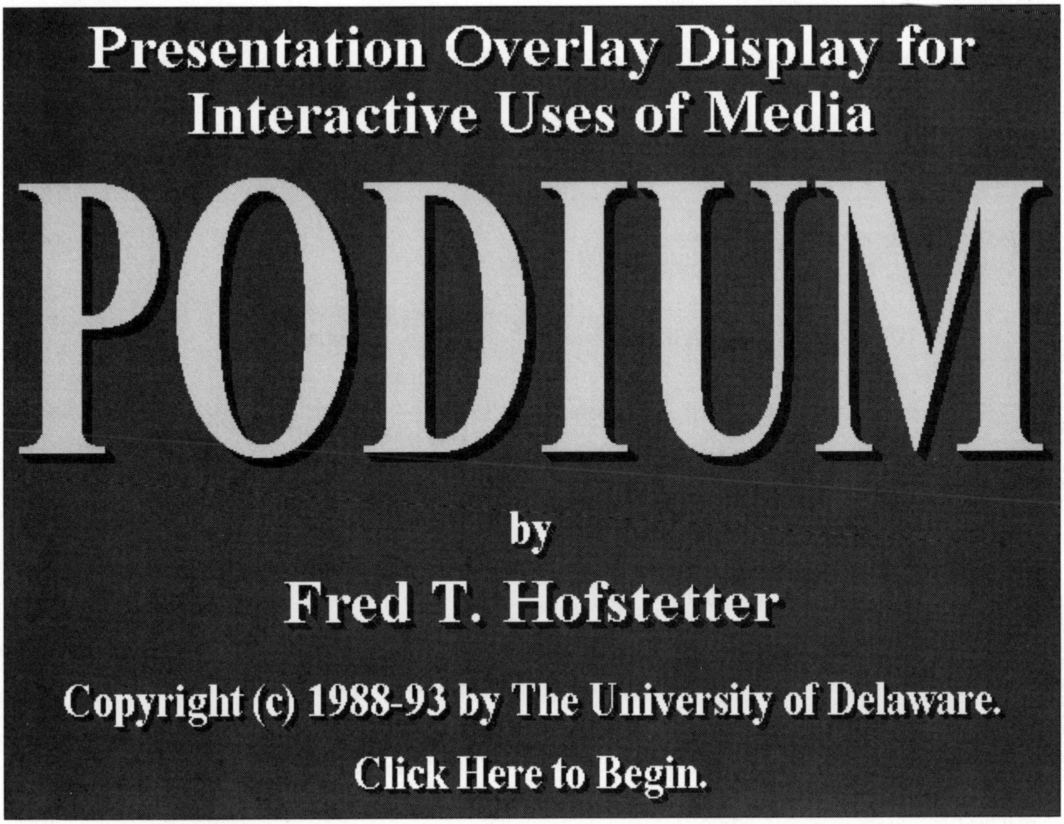

Presentation Overlay Display for Interactive Uses of Media

PODIUM

by

Fred T. Hofstetter

Copyright (c) 1988-93 by The University of Delaware.

Click Here to Begin.

FIGURE 11.1
PODIUM title screen.

Previewing the TQM Presentation

For those readers taking an armchair approach to the tutorial, or for those who would like to preview the TQM presentation before working through the tutorial, you will find it listed on the last page of the PODIUM demonstration menu. While running the PODIUM demonstration, simply press the PageDown key until you see Total Quality Management Tutorial, and then click on it. Try each item in the TQM presentation to find out what it does.

Readers who plan to work through the tutorial and actually complete the exercises in this book should delete the TQM files on their hard drives before proceeding. DOS users will find the TQM files in their \PODIUM\TQM directory; Windows users will find them in \WNPODIUM\TQM; and OS/2 users will find them in \PMPODIUM\TQM. Assuming your hard drive is C, type one of the following:

DOS users:	del c:\podium\tqm*.*
Windows:	del c:\wnpodium\tqm*.*
OS/2 users:	del c:\pmpodium\tqm*.*

Chapter 12

Planning the Total Quality Management Presentation

When planning a presentation, you begin by making a list of what you want to present. If you do this on paper, you can be frustrated when you think of an item that should have gone before one you already wrote down. If you use a text editor or word processor to create the list, you can easily insert new ideas where they belong. Moreover, if you decide an item you typed earlier should be moved up or down in the list, you can use the cut, copy, and paste tools in your text editor to move the text and "shape" your presentation into a form that fits your plan.

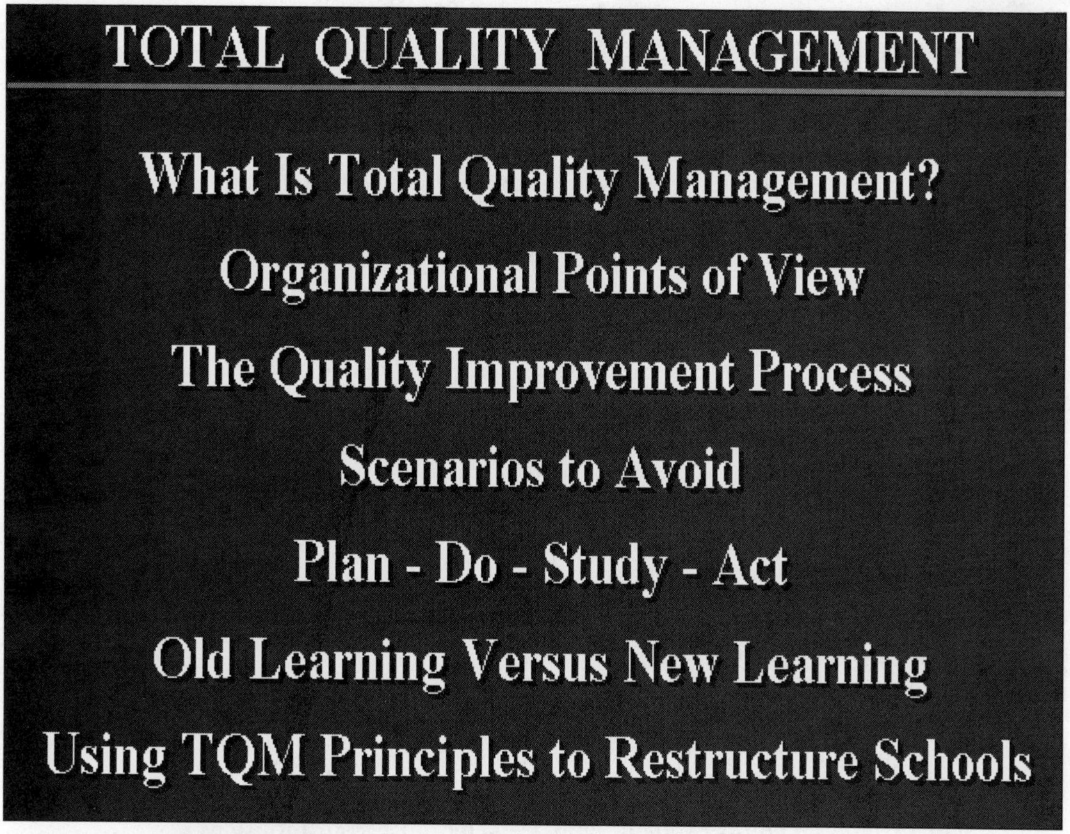

TOTAL QUALITY MANAGEMENT

What Is Total Quality Management?

Organizational Points of View

The Quality Improvement Process

Scenarios to Avoid

Plan - Do - Study - Act

Old Learning Versus New Learning

Using TQM Principles to Restructure Schools

FIGURE 12.1
The seven main points of the TQM presentation.

The TQM presentation you create in this tutorial has the seven main points listed in Figure 12.1.

Each point is listed on the home bullet file with which the TQM presentation begins. You learn how to link each point to other presentation files and multimedia objects used to explain it. The tutorial has been designed so each point also teaches you a different presentation technique. The following sections summarize what each point teaches you. The tutorial steps you through the creation of each point, allowing you to work at your own pace as you gradually build an effective presentation of TQM.

What Is Total Quality Management?

With the first point you learn how to create hypertext by linking a line of text to secondary text. The secondary text contains the definition of TQM. Any time you want to show the definition of TQM, you click with your mouse on "What is Total Quality Management?" and the definition instantly appears. As a special touch, you also learn how to underlay your presentation bullets with a bitmap. For this purpose, a TQM logo bitmap has been provided for you to use as a backdrop. You will probably want to use this simple yet effective backdrop technique in all your home presentation files.

Organizational Points of View

The second point illustrates how easy it is to flow images onto the screen with PODIUM. By linking two bitmaps to the bullet titled "Organizational Points of View," you are able to use your mouse to make a graphical comparison of the traditional hierarchical viewpoint with the systems viewpoint used in TQM.

The Quality Improvement Process

McCormack (1992) identifies eight strategic steps in the quality improvement process. You make a hyperbullet slide that lists these eight steps; then you create slides that explain each step and link them to the hyperbullet slide. Anytime you want to show one of the steps in the quality improvement process, you are just a mouse click away from it.

Scenarios to Avoid

As McCormack (1992) cautions, there are three scenarios you must be careful to avoid in attempting to use TQM. You make three text slides that explain these scenarios and then link them to the bullet "Scenarios to Avoid." Clicking on this bullet launches a virtual slide tray containing the three slides. You learn how to use your mouse like a 35-mm slide control to move back and forth through the scenarios as you warn your audience to avoid them.

Plan—Do—Study—Act

The fifth point provides you an opportunity to learn how to make hyperpictures. You create a trigger file that displays a diagram of the Plan—Do—Study—Act cycle used in TQM. Then you link explanations of each step in the cycle to the part of the picture that pertains to it. During your presentation when you decide to explain this diagram, you click on each of these four triggers to launch an explanation.

Old Learning Versus New Learning

The sixth point demonstrates PODIUM's ability to create columns in your presentation slides and lets you build a slide with your mouse. As you click your mouse to build the slide, PODIUM prints an attribute of traditional education in the first column and its TQM interpretation in the second. The technique of showing contrasts, comparing something new to something familiar, is an effective way to help someone learn a new concept.

Using TQM Principles to Restructure Schools

The last point shows how to create a bullet slide that builds. Each time you click your mouse on the bullet slide, PODIUM reveals one more technique for using TQM principles to restructure schools.

TQM Presentation Concept Map

Sometimes it is helpful to draw a diagram of the presentation you want to create. Figure 12.2 provides such a diagram of the TQM presentation that you create for this tutorial. While this may look complicated at first, the tutorial steps you through each point and shows how easy it is to create such a dynamic multimedia presentation.

TQM Acknowledgments

The author wishes to acknowledge two TQM practitioners who granted permission for some of their materials to be used in this book. Shaun P. McCormack of Management Effectiveness Corporation developed the eight strategic steps for TQM and gave permission to quote them in this tutorial; he also identified and granted permission to quote the three scenarios to avoid.

Professor John Cleveland of Grand Rapids Community College conducts workshops on using TQM to restructure schools. He granted permission for this book to include several materials from his workshop, including the definition of TQM, the two diagrams of organizational viewpoints, the Plan—Do—Study—Act process, the old learning versus new learning contrasts, and using TQM principles to restructure schools.

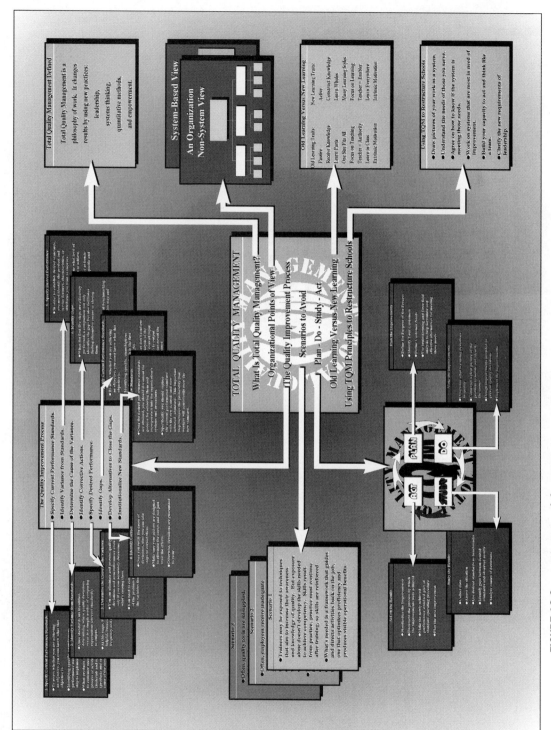

FIGURE 12.2 Diagram of the TQM presentation.

Chapter 13

Creating the Home Bullet File

H aving studied the plan for the TQM presentation, it is now time to get down to business and create it on your computer. First create a TQM directory on your hard disk drive to hold your TQM presentation. Assuming your hard drive is C, the command to type is

    md c:\tqm

Making Bullets in the Home File

The home file for the TQM tutorial appears in Figure 13.1. If you are doing the hands-on tutorial, use your text editor or word processor to type this exactly as you see it. Save the file in your TQM directory as TQM.BUL. The .BUL file extension stands for

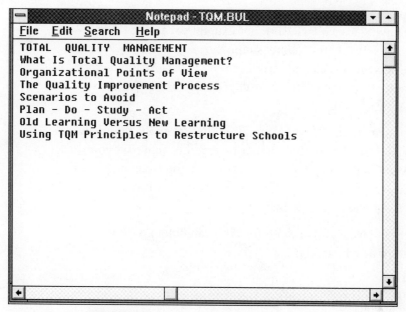

FIGURE 13.1
The home bullet file TQM.BUL.

bullet. Be sure to save the file in ASCII format. If your text editor has no options for file formats, it probably uses ASCII by default. Some helpful tips for editing PODIUM presentation files follow.

Tips for DOS Users
Many DOS users like to use *WordPerfect* with PODIUM. To make *WordPerfect* save files in the ASCII format, save your files using CTRL-F5, and choose the DOS Text format. Because using *WordPerfect* requires that you exit PODIUM each time you want to use *WordPerfect* to edit your presentation file, to try it with PODIUM you must exit *WordPerfect*. Starting and exiting programs is time-consuming.

There is a much easier and quicker way to edit PODIUM for DOS presentations by using the text editor that comes with *SideKick*. *SideKick* is a memory-resident desktop accessory that contains tools like a calculator, a phone directory, a calendar, and a text editor called a Notepad. If you load *SideKick* before executing the PODIUM program, you can hot key in and out of Notepad while

PODIUM is running. This allows you to edit a presentation file without having to exit PODIUM. For example, if a slide takes longer to dissolve than you like, simply hot key into *SideKick* and adjust it. To switch back and forth between PODIUM and *SideKick*, simply hold down the CTRL key and press the ALT key; this is called a Control-ALT.

Changes made to PODIUM presentation files take effect immediately unless you change the file that is currently active on your PODIUM display. To see the new version, use the Done button to leave the presentation file, and then retrigger it, or use the Reread option (R) to reload the file instantly.

SideKick is published by Borland Inc. You can obtain ordering information by contacting

Borland Inc.
1800 Green Hills Road
P.O. Box 660001
Scotts Valley, CA 95066-0001

Make sure you get *SideKick* version 2.0 or later. Earlier versions will stripe the top of the PODIUM display. When this happens, you can press R to make PODIUM refresh the screen.

Tips for Windows and OS/2 Users

Windows and OS/2 users can use any text editor or word processor concurrently with PODIUM. Simply use your task manager to move back and forth between PODIUM and your text file.

The fastest way to create a new file or edit an existing one is to use the Create New and Edit options from the PODIUM Files menu. They spawn text editing windows that consist of Notepad for Windows and the enhanced system editor for OS/2.

There are two ways to get PODIUM to display your TQM.BUL file. You can give PODIUM a start-up parameter that makes it automatically begin with the TQM.BUL file, or you can use the PODIUM Files feature to select TQM.BUL.

Start-up Instructions for DOS Users

If you are using PODIUM for DOS and you want to make PODIUM start with the TQM.BUL file, type the following command from your DOS prompt (this assumes that your hard drive is C):

    c:\podium\podemo.exe c:\tqm\tqm.bul

If you are already running PODIUM for DOS and you want to switch to the TQM.BUL file, press the F4 function key, type in your TQM directory, click on BUL files, and choose TQM.BUL. (Anytime you want to see what function keys are available in PODIUM for DOS, press the F1 function key.)

Start-up Instructions for Windows Users

To make PODIUM for Windows begin with the TQM.BUL file, change the properties of the PODIUM icon as follows. First, click once with your left mouse button on the PODIUM icon to select it. Now pull down the File menu and choose Properties. In the Properties window, click on the command line field, and edit it by adding the name of the TQM.BUL file, making the command line read as follows:

    c:\wnpodium\wnpodemo.exe c:\tqm\tqm.bul

Click on OK to close the Properties window. When you double-click on the PODIUM icon, it will automatically start with the TQM presentation.

Start-up Instructions for OS/2 Users

There are two ways to make PODIUM for Presentation Manager start up with the TQM.BUL file. You can start PODIUM from an OS/2 full-screen prompt by typing

    c:\pmpodium\pmpodemo.exe c:\tqm\tqm.bul

or you can modify the PODIUM icon so that when you click on it, the TQM.BUL file will start. To do this, click with your right mouse button on the PODIUM icon and choose Open; then choose Settings. In the optional parameters field, erase any text it may already contain, and type

    c:\tqm\tqm.bul

Close Settings by double-clicking on the little PODIUM icon in the upper left corner of the Settings window. Now when you double-click on the PODIUM icon, it will automatically start with the TQM presentation.

The Retail PODIUM Message

If the file you type does not closely resemble the one in Figure 13.1, PODIUM will think you are trying to create a different presentation, and it will display a polite message informing you that you need a retail copy in order to create your own customized presentations.

Adding a TQM Underlay

A very effective technique in PODIUM is to underlay your presentation bullets with a picture or graphic. For example, there is a TQM logo in the PODIUM directories. To underlay your presentation bullets with it, simply insert the following line at the very top of your presentation file:

DOS USERS   **WINDOWS AND OS/2 USERS**
! tqm.pcx   ! tqm.bmp

Your presentation file should now read like Figure 13.2, in which the underlay line has been highlighted.

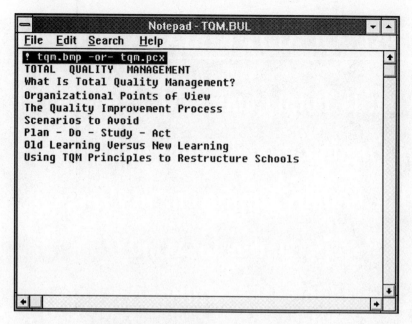

FIGURE 13.2
Adding a TQM backdrop.

Make sure you save the file with your text editor. When you return to PODIUM, the change will automatically take effect for Windows and OS/2 users. DOS users must press the R key in order for the change to take effect; R stands for Read and forces PODIUM to reread your current presentation file.

Figure 13.3 shows how the TQM logo now beautifully underlays the presentation bullets and makes your presentation more interesting than it would be if you had only text. This process is so easy, yet it makes your slides so much more effective. With PODIUM you can underlay any picture from any source. For example, you could underlay your corporate logo or school coat of arms, or a picture of your headquarters, or a photo of what you are proposing to build or seeking to have funded.

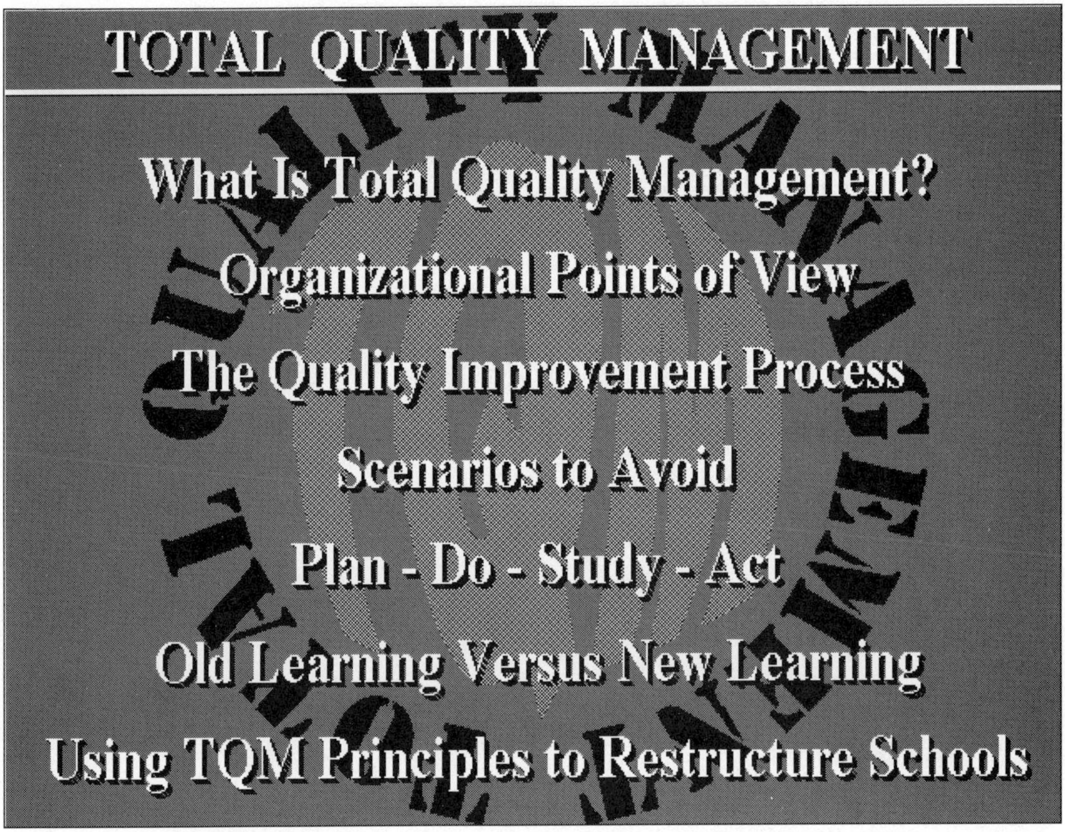

FIGURE 13.3
The TQM logo underlays the TQM home file.

Chapter 14

Defining Total Quality Management

T he first bullet in the TQM home file refers to the definition of TQM. The steps ahead show how to create a bullet file that defines TQM and how to link it to the first bullet of the TQM.BUL file. When you click with your mouse on the bullet titled "What Is Total Quality Management," the definition will instantly appear.

Creating a Secondary Bullet File

Secondary bullet files are created the same way you made the home bullet file: you simply type them with any text editor and

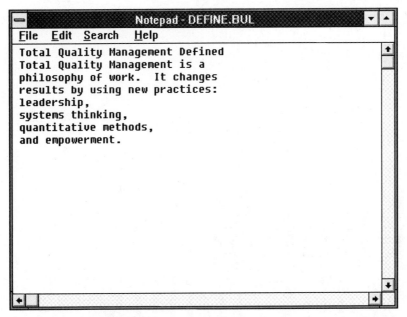

FIGURE 14.1
Definition of TQM.

save them in ASCII format with a .BUL file extension. In fact, all bullet files are made this way.

The text of the definition for TQM appears in Figure 14.1. Using your text editor, type the text exactly as you see it in the figure; then save the file in your TQM directory under the name DEFINE.BUL.

Linking the Definition

To link the definition to the "What Is Total Quality Management" bullet, edit your TQM.BUL file and insert the following line immediately after the bullet:

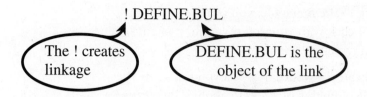

! DEFINE.BUL

The ! creates linkage

DEFINE.BUL is the object of the link

Save your DEFINE.BUL file. It should now appear as shown in Figure 14.2, which highlights the inserted line.

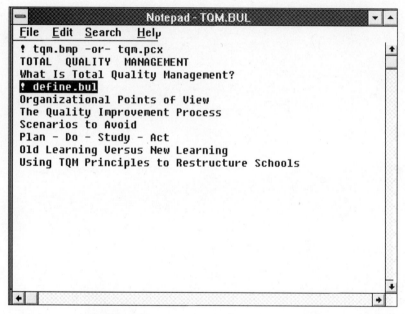

```
┌─────────────────────────────────────────────────────┐
│ ─      Notepad - TQM.BUL              ▼  ▲           │
├─────────────────────────────────────────────────────┤
│ File  Edit  Search  Help                             │
├─────────────────────────────────────────────────────┤
│ ! tqm.bmp -or- tqm.pcx                          ↑    │
│ TOTAL   QUALITY   MANAGEMENT                          │
│ What Is Total Quality Management?                     │
│ ! define.bul                                         │
│ Organizational Points of View                        │
│ The Quality Improvement Process                      │
│ Scenarios to Avoid                                   │
│ Plan - Do - Study - Act                              │
│ Old Learning Versus New Learning                     │
│ Using TQM Principles to Restructure Schools          │
│                                                 ↓    │
│ ←                                               →    │
└─────────────────────────────────────────────────────┘
```

FIGURE 14.2
Linking the definition of TQM.

Navigating the Linkage

Navigating the linkage could not be easier. Simply click with your mouse anywhere on the text of the first bullet, "What Is Total Quality Management," and PODIUM will instantly display the definition for you. To return to the home file, you can press F3 for DONE, F9 for HOME, or click with your left mouse button anywhere on the definition screen.

Practice this linkage repeatedly. Notice how fast you can show the definition. This principle of linking one text to another by means of the exclamation point can give you the same instant access to any corporate data, instructional text, or information you enter with any text editor.

Chapter 15

Bitmapped Illustrations of Organizational Style

I t has often been said that a picture is worth a thousand words. Two bitmaps in your PODIUM directory will help your audience visualize the TQM process. One shows the traditional hierarchical organization that most companies and schools use today; the second shows how the TQM process encourages people to think of an organization according to the flow of ideas and processes—instead of who reports to whom.

Linking Bitmaps to Bullets

Let's begin by linking the traditional organizational viewpoint to the bullet titled "Organizational Points of View." The name of the bitmap is NONSYS.PCX for DOS users and NONSYS.BMP for Windows and OS/2 users. To link it to the bullet for "Organizational Points of View," edit the file TQM.BUL by inserting the following line immediately after "Organizational Points of View":

DOS USERS	WINDOWS AND OS/2 USERS
! nonsys.pcx	! nonsys.bmp

Save your file and return to PODIUM. Now when you click on the bullet for "Organizational Points of View," you will see the traditional organizational viewpoint. To return to your bullets, click with your left mouse button anywhere on the organizational chart, or press F3 (DONE) or F9 (HOME).

Creating a Virtual Slide Tray

So far, clicking on the bullet titled "Organizational Points of View" shows only one slide because you linked only one slide to it. To add another slide, enter another link. For example, there is a bitmap that shows how organizations are viewed in the TQM process. It is called SYSTEM.PCX for DOS users and SYSTEM.BMP for Windows and OS/2 users. To make it appear in sequence right after you show the traditional organizational viewpoint, insert the following line immediately beneath your NONSYS image:

DOS USERS	WINDOWS AND OS/2 USERS
! system.pcx	! system.bmp

SAVE your TQM.BUL file. It should now appear as shown in Figure 15.1 in which the two organizational bitmaps have been highlighted.

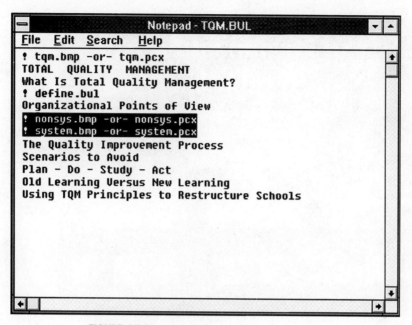

FIGURE 15.1

TQM.BUL linked to hierarchical and systematical
organizational viewpoints.

In PODIUM, click with your mouse on the bullet for "Organizational Points of View," and you will first see the nonsystematic
viewpoint, as shown in Figure 15.2. Now click with your left
mouse button anywhere on the picture, and you will get the next
slide, as shown in Figure 15.3, showing the systematic viewpoint.
Notice how quickly the second slide appeared. That is because
while you were viewing the first slide, PODIUM loaded the second
one so it would appear as soon as you clicked your left mouse button. To return to the first slide, click your right mouse button anywhere on the second slide. In PODIUM, your mouse works just
like a 35-mm slide projector: the left button takes you forward to
the next slide, and the right button takes you back to the previous
slide.

These two images now work like slides in a 35-mm slide tray.
However, instead of being limited to showing them in a predetermined order at a predetermined time, you can use your text editor

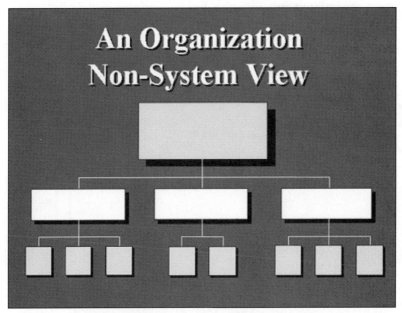

FIGURE 15.2
The NONSYS.BMP file as a slide.

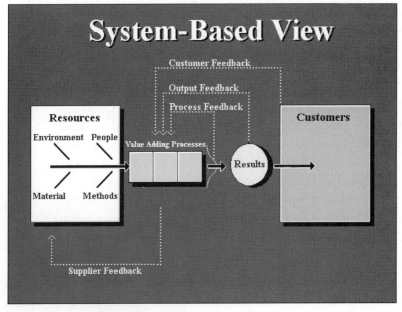

FIGURE 15.3
The SYSTEM.BMP file as a slide.

to put these slides in any order you want, have as many slides as you want in the tray, and be able to return at any time to your presentation bullets from which you could choose another tray of slides. PODIUM's capability to show any slide, any text, any multimedia object at any time is its most powerful feature.

To return to your bullets press F3 (DONE) or F9 (HOME) anytime, or click your left mouse button on the last slide in the tray. Notice how PODIUM now gives you the option of clicking on the first bullet, "What Is Total Quality Management," to see the TQM definition or on the bullet titled "Organizational Points of View" to show the two opposing organizational viewpoints. Practice navigating these links and think about the power this will give you as a presenter.

Indeed, we find that the old saying a picture is worth a thousand words merits the following adaptation: A picture is worth a thousand words if you can show it when you need it. With PODIUM, you can show any picture anytime. You literally can have access to thousands of slides within a second.

Dissolve Patterns and Transition Effects

When you show the two organizational viewpoints, they appear with PODIUM's default dissolve pattern and timing. By adding PODIUM special effects, you can change the pattern with which images dissolve onto the screen, and you can make the dissolve take more or less time depending on the effect you want to achieve.

DOS users need to enter the dissolve effects by editing their presentation file manually. Windows and OS/2 users can either do likewise or use the PODIUM Effects menu, which makes the edits for you. While viewing a slide in PODIUM, pull down the Effects menu and choose the effect you want; PODIUM automatically edits your presentation file, inserting the special effect so you do not need to type it in manually.

Take a few minutes now to experiment with the PODIUM dissolve and timing effects. For example, try making these edits, save your file, and show the pictures to see the effects these dissolve patterns make. Notice how PODIUM special effects always begin with an @ sign.

DOS USERS
! nonsys.pcx @method=stripes @direction=down @time=2
! system.pcx @method=replace @direction=up @time=3

! nonsys.pcx @method=split @direction=up @time=1.5
! system.pcx @method=split @direction=down @time=1.5

WINDOWS AND OS/2 USERS
! nonsys.bmp @method=stripes @direction=down @time=2
! system.bmp @method=replace @direction=up @time=3

! nonsys.bmp @method=split @direction=up @time=1.5
! system.bmp @method=split @direction=down @time=1.5

As you see, the method can be stripes, replace, or split; the direction can be up or down; and the time can be any whole number or decimal. The longer the time, the longer it will take for your image to dissolve onto the screen. Try using your right mouse button while viewing the second image and see how the first image dissolves over it when PODIUM backs up in your virtual slide tray.

Advantages of the PODIUM Effects Menu

PODIUM's Effects menu is context-sensitive, meaning that its contents change depending on what you are doing. For example, Figure 15.4 shows the result of pulling down the Effects menu while PODIUM is displaying a picture. To add a special effect to a picture, you simply choose the one you want, and PODIUM edits your presentation file automatically, saving you the time needed to edit it by hand.

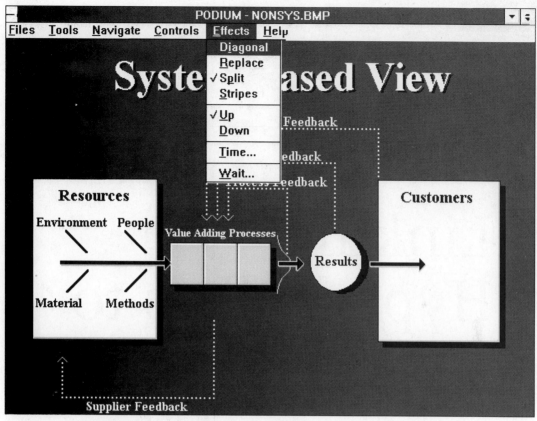

FIGURE 15.4
Appearance of Effects menu when PODIUM is displaying a picture.

DOS users who have upgraded to the Windows version of PODIUM tell how the Effects menu makes PODIUM a hundred times easier to use. Indeed, getting the Effects menu is another good reason for DOS users to upgrade to Windows.

Chapter 16

Linking Hyperbullets to Hyperbullets

The number of linkages you can make with PODIUM is unlimited. Any object can be linked to any other object any number of times. To illustrate this we will now create a hyperbullet slide, link it to a bullet in the TQM.BUL file, and link each one of its bullets to another slide. By completing this example, you will see how easy this is and yet how infinitely powerful it will make your presentations.

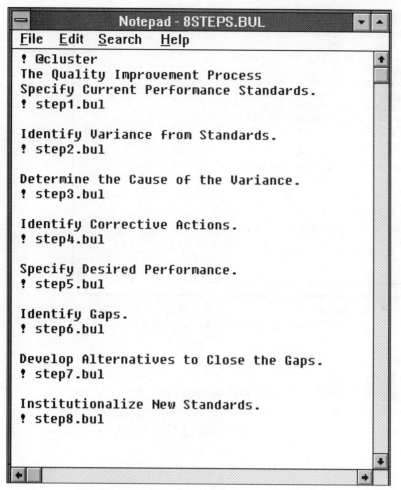

FIGURE 16.1

Eight steps involved in building a strategic TQM framework.

The Quality Improvement Process

Let us begin by creating a new bullet file called 8STEPS.BUL. We call it 8STEPS.BUL because of the eight steps involved in building a strategic TQM framework.

The file to type appears in Figure 16.1. Notice how it uses the @cluster style and contains linkages to eight more bullet files,

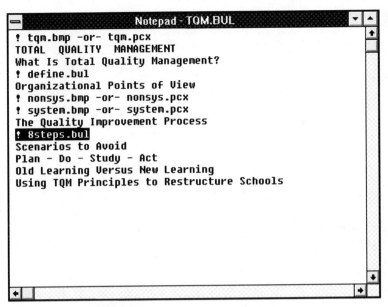

```
┌──────────────────────────────────────────────┬───┬───┐
│ ─            Notepad - TQM.BUL                │ ▼ │ ▲ │
├──────────────────────────────────────────────┴───┴───┤
│ ! tqm.bmp -or- tqm.pcx                              │▲│
│ TOTAL  QUALITY  MANAGEMENT                           │ │
│ What Is Total Quality Management?                   │ │
│ ! define.bul                                        │ │
│ Organizational Points of View                       │ │
│ ! nonsys.bmp -or- nonsys.pcx                         │ │
│ ! system.bmp -or- system.pcx                         │ │
│ The Quality Improvement Process                     │ │
│ ▐! 8steps.bul▌                                       │ │
│ Scenarios to Avoid                                  │ │
│ Plan - Do - Study - Act                             │ │
│ Old Learning Versus New Learning                    │ │
│ Using TQM Principles to Restructure Schools         │ │
│                                                     │ │
│                                                     │ │
│                                                     │▼│
│ ◄ ░                                              ► │
└──────────────────────────────────────────────────────┘
```

FIGURE 16.2
TQM.BUL linked to eight quality management steps.

which you will create later. Go ahead and type the linkages exactly as they appear in Figure 16.1. Be sure to insert the blank lines in Figure 16.1; they tell PODIUM where your clusters end. When you are finished, save the file in ASCII format as 8STEPS.BUL.

Linking the TQM Process to Its Hyperbullet

To link 8STEPS.BUL to the hyperbullet that will trigger it, edit the file TQM.BUL, inserting the line highlighted in Figure 16.2, and then save the TQM.BUL file. If you run PODIUM now and click with your mouse on the bullet titled "The Quality Improvement Process," you will see your eight steps. Now try clicking on any one of the eight steps. Because you have not yet created the eight bullet files to which these steps will be linked, PODIUM cannot find them. A message to this effect appears, and then you are per-

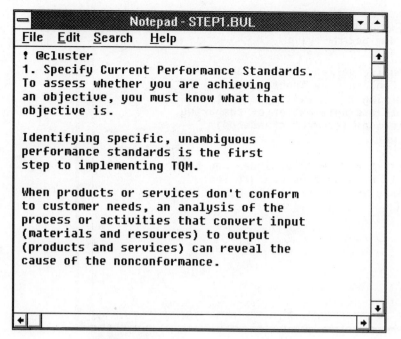

FIGURE 16.3
Step 1 in the TQM framework: STEP1.BUL.

mitted to continue running PODIUM as usual. Read on to create the eight bullet files.

Eight Steps in the TQM Framework

Figures 16.3 through 16.10 show the eight BUL files that describe the eight steps in the TQM framework. They are named STEP1.BUL through STEP8.BUL, respectively. If you would prefer not to spend time typing them, you can find them in the TQM directory on your CD-ROM. Instead of typing them, you can copy them by entering the following command:

```
copy d:\tqm\step*.bul c:\tqm
```

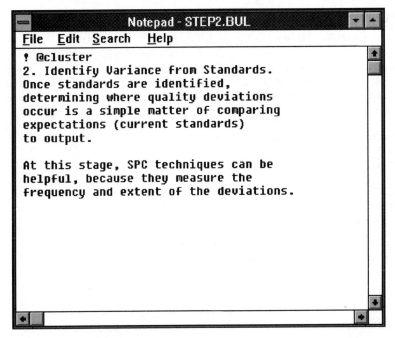

FIGURE 16.4
Step 2 in the TQM framework: STEP2.BUL.

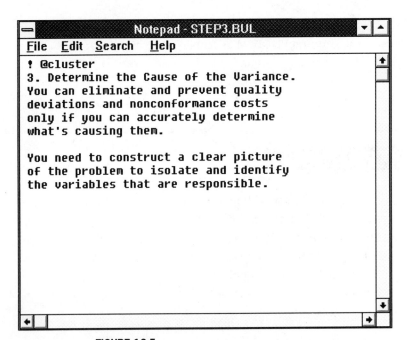

FIGURE 16.5
Step 3 in the TQM framework: STEP3.BUL.

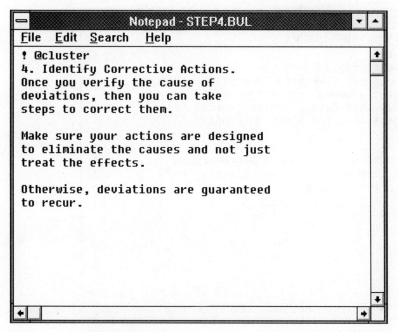

FIGURE 16.6
Step 4 in the TQM framework: STEP4.BUL.

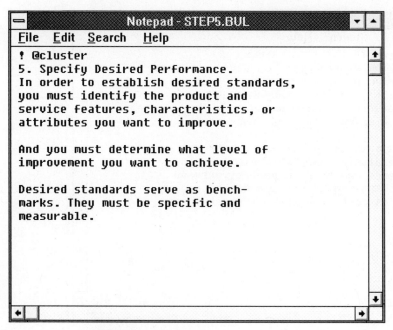

FIGURE 16.7
Step 5 in the TQM framework: STEP5.BUL.

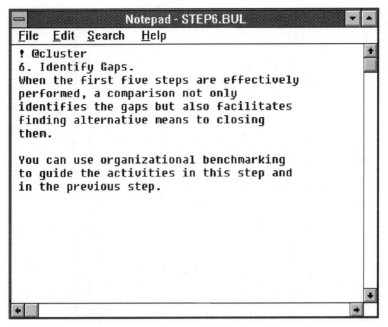

FIGURE 16.8
Step 6 in the TQM framework: STEP6.BUL.

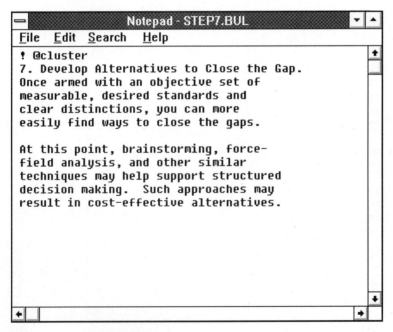

FIGURE 16.9
Step 7 in the TQM framework: STEP7.BUL.

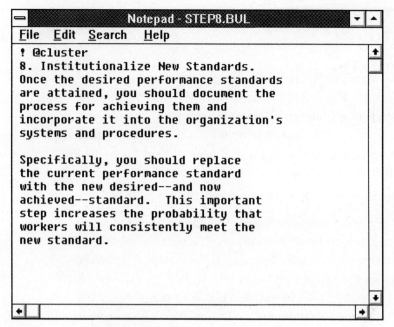

FIGURE 16.10
Step 8 in the TQM framework: STEP8.BUL.

Navigating the Eight-Step Links

Now when you run your TQM presentation with PODIUM and click on the bullets in the 8STEPS.BUL file, PODIUM will instantly display the bullet file that you linked to that step. Click on each bullet in 8STEPS.BUL to make sure its linkage works. While viewing each step, you can either press F3 for DONE or click with your left mouse button anywhere in the PODIUM window to return to the 8STEPS.BUL file; pressing F9 for HOME will take you back to the TQM.BUL file.

Practice navigating. Notice how you can show any part of your presentation whenever you want. For example, at any time you can press F9 to return home and then show the organizational bitmaps or the definition of TQM. If someone asked you a question pertaining to one of those items, you could use PODIUM to show it instantly.

Color Selection

If you have Windows or OS/2 and you pull down the Effects menu while viewing one of the eight-step bullet files, the choices will permit you to change the color of the foreground text and the background screen that appears behind it. DOS users must make color changes by hand by inserting at the very top of the bullet file a line such as the following:

! @foreground=yellow @background=black

You must be careful choosing foreground and background colors because some project better than others. The best choice, white foreground text on a blue background, is the PODIUM default; if you do not set the colors for a bullet or text slide, you will get white text on a blue background. Red text does not project well. Dark blue is a good substitute for the normal blue background to which PODIUM defaults. In general, make sure your foreground color provides a good contrast to the background color in your slide. Avoid bright backgrounds like yellow or white unless you are trying to achieve some special effect.

Chapter 17

Text Files as Slides

The fourth bullet in the TQM.BUL file is titled "Scenarios to Avoid." There are three such scenarios, each one described in its own text file.

Creating Three Scenarios to Avoid

The three text files pictured in Figures 17.1, 17.2, and 17.3 are named SCENE1.BUL, SCENE2.BUL, and SCENE3.BUL, respectively. You can either type these into your text editor and save them using these names or copy them from your CD-ROM by typing the following:

```
copy d:\tqm\scene*.bul c:\tqm
```

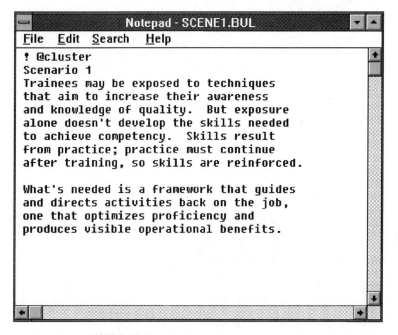

FIGURE 17.1
Scenario 1: SCENE1.BUL.

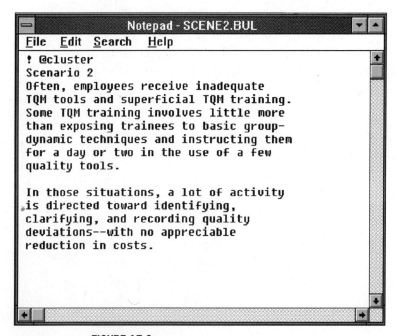

FIGURE 17.2
Scenario 2: SCENE2.BUL.

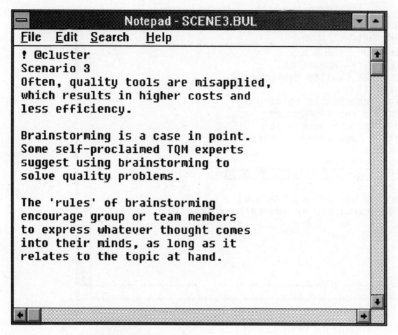

FIGURE 17.3
Scenario 3: SCENE3.BUL.

Linking TQM Scenarios to Avoid

It is easy to link these three scenario files to the bullet that will trigger them, "Scenarios to Avoid." To create such a linkage, edit the TQM.BUL file, inserting the line highlighted in Figure 17.4.

Now when you run your presentation and click on the bullet for "Scenarios to Avoid," you will see SCENE1.BUL; click anywhere on it with your left mouse button to advance to SCENE2.BUL. Click again with your left mouse button to advance to SCENE3.BUL. A right mouse click will move back one scenario. To return to the TQM.BUL slide, press F3 (DONE) or F9 (HOME), or click with your left mouse button anywhere on the third scenario slide.

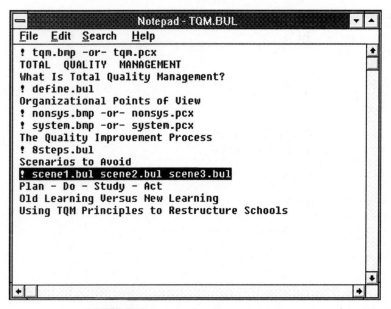

FIGURE 17.4
Linking the three scenarios to avoid.

Chapter 18

Total Quality Management Picture Menu

So far, all of the objects in your TQM presentation have been triggered by clicking with your mouse on lines of hypertext. PODIUM has another way of triggering events; it is called the trigger file. Trigger files let you display a picture and overlay invisible triggers on it. There is no limit to the number of triggers you can have, and each one can trigger any multimedia object or list of objects on your computer.

Just as the names of bullet files end with .BUL, trigger filenames end with a .TRI file extension. The trigger file you create will be called CYCLE.TRI. During your presentation it will appear when you click with your mouse on the bullet titled "Plan—Do—Study—Act" in your TQM.BUL file. To create that linkage, edit your TQM.BUL file and insert the line highlighted in Figure 18.1.

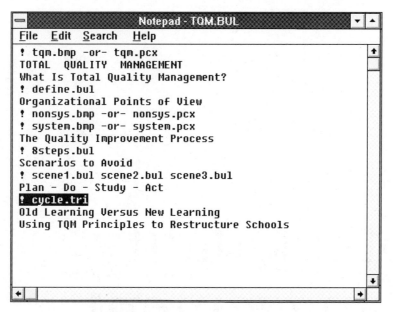

FIGURE 18.1
Linking "Plan—Do—Study—Act" to a TQM trigger file.

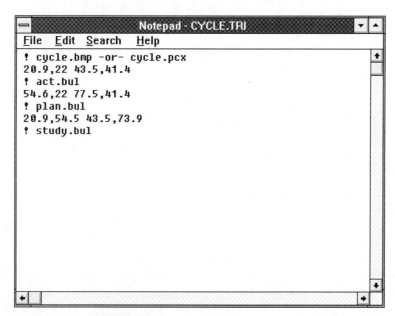

FIGURE 18.2
Creating the first three triggers in CYCLE.TRI.

Save the TQM.BUL file and run it with PODIUM. When you click on the bullet titled "Plan—Do—Study—Act," you will get a message that PODIUM cannot find the CYCLE.TRI file; that is because you have not yet created it. We do that in the next section.

Creating Trigger Files

You can use any text editor or word processor to create a trigger file. You begin by typing a link to the image on which the triggers will be overlaid. Then specify the x,y coordinates of each trigger to which you link the object(s) you want to be triggered. Accordingly, trigger files have the following format:

```
! bitmapped image or videodisc frame upon which
! triggers will be placed
x1,y1 x2,y2 (coordinates of the first trigger)
! object -or- objectlist
! objectlist (continued; use as many ! lines as needed)
x1,y1 x2,y2 (coordinates of the second trigger)
! object -or- objectlist
! objectlist (continued; use as many ! lines as needed)
x1,y1 x2,y2 (coordinates of the third trigger)
 .
 .
 .
```

(continue for as many x,y coordinates as you want)

To get you started creating the TQM trigger file, use your text editor to create a new file that contains the seven lines of text shown on the previous page in Figure 18.2.

Save the file, giving it the filename CYCLE.TRI. Now run your TQM.BUL presentation with PODIUM, and click on the bullet titled "Plan—Do—Study—Act." Notice how the TQM cycle bitmap appears on your screen.

Interacting with the TQM Trigger File

Now press the F11 function key. This is PODIUM's Show Triggers tool. Windows and OS/2 users can also access this tool by pulling down the Tools menu and selecting Show Triggers; DOS users can always find out what key to select by pressing F1.

Press the F11 key again, and the triggers will disappear. Pressing it a third time will show the triggers again. F11 acts as a toggle that either lights or erases the edges of the triggers.

Now click on the part of the bitmap where one of the triggers is located. Whether or not you have the trigger highlighted, you see how it triggers the file you linked to it when you created the CYCLE.TRI file. Because you have not yet created those files, PODIUM will display a message informing you that they cannot be found. We will create those files a little later; first you learn how to make a trigger by creating one for the word *act* in the CYCLE.TRI file.

Making Triggers

Each trigger has the following form:

```
x1,y1 x2,y2
! object -or- objectlist
! objectlist (continued; use as many ! lines as needed)
```

The triggers are rectangular and are defined by *x1,y1* and *x2,y2*. The top left coordinate of the trigger is *x1,y1*, and the bottom right is *x2,y2*. If you study the diagram in Figure 18.3, you will understand how each pair of coordinates tells PODIUM how far over (*x*) and how far down (*y*) to put the trigger. Each number is a percentage. For example, the trigger locations 20.9,22 43.5,41.4 tell PODIUM to make a trigger whose upper left corner is 20.9% over and 22% down the screen, with its lower right corner 43.5% over and 41.4% down the screen.

FIGURE 18.3
The x,y coordinates of the first three triggers in CYCLE.TRI.

The x,y Tool

To create a trigger, you must find out what its *x,y* coordinates will
be. PODIUM makes this easy by providing the *x,y* Tool that you can
use to determine the *x,y* coordinates of any point on the screen.
Windows and OS/2 users activate this tool by pulling down the
Tools menu and selecting *x,y* Tool. DOS users activate it by pressing
the F4 function key and selecting the image type, which in this
case is PCX.

Creating the Fourth TQM Trigger

Now you will see how easy it is to create a trigger by adding the fourth trigger to the CYCLE.TRI file. First, you must determine its *x,y* location and make the corresponding edit in the CYCLE.TRI file. While viewing CYCLE.TRI with PODIUM, activate the *x,y* Tool, and click with your mouse on the upper left corner of the word *ACT*. PODIUM will tell you the *x,y* values of that point. If you are using Windows or OS/2, PODIUM copies that point to your clipboard from which you can paste it into your CYCLE.TRI file with your text editor. If you are using PODIUM for DOS, you must make the edit manually.

Now you repeat this process for the lower right corner of the trigger. In PODIUM with the *x,y* Tool activated, click on the lower right corner of the word *ACT*, and insert those coordinates into CYCLE.TRI. Figure 18.4 highlights these coordinates. Do not be too concerned if your *x,y* coordinates are not exactly the same as those shown in Figure 18.4. They should, however, be close to those values.

Linking Objects to Triggers

To complete CYCLE.TRI, you link the file DO.BUL to the trigger you just created. Links to triggers are made exactly the same way you link objects to text: type an exclamation point in the first column of the line beneath the trigger, and then type the object(s) you want to link. Figure 18.4 shows CYCLE.TRI with the link to DO.BUL. Use your text editor or word processor to create this linkage now. Save the file and press F11 in PODIUM to see the trigger you added.

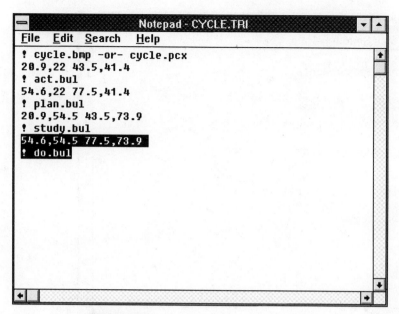

FIGURE 18.4
CYCLE.TRI with the fourth trigger inserted.

Creating the Plan—Do—Study—Act Files

If you click on a trigger in the CYCLE.TRI file, PODIUM will tell
you it cannot find the object to which you linked it. It is time to
create those now. They are listed in Figures 18.5 through 18.8. Use
your text editor to create them, and save them in your TQM directory. To save time, you can copy them from the PODIUM CD-ROM
by typing the following:

```
copy    d:\tqm\plan.bul    c:\tqm
copy    d:\tqm\do.bul      c:\tqm
copy    d:\tqm\study.bul   c:\tqm
copy    d:\tqm\act.bul     c:\tqm
```

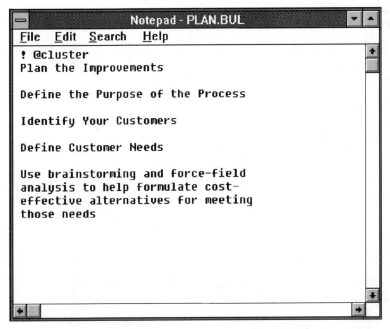

FIGURE 18.5
The PLAN.BUL file.

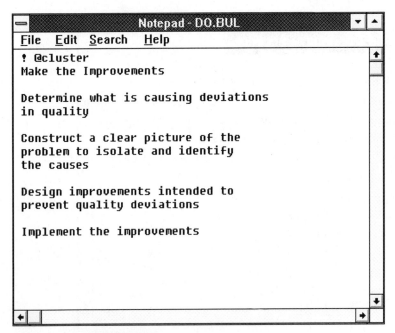

FIGURE 18.6
The DO.BUL file.

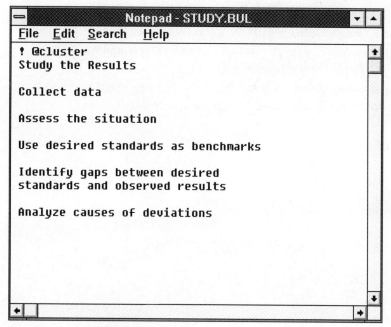

FIGURE 18.7
The STUDY.BUL file.

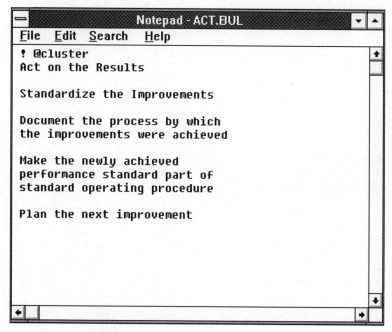

FIGURE 18.8
The ACT.BUL file.

Try clicking on each of the four triggers in CYCLE.TRI to see how PODIUM handles the linkages. Spend a few moments thinking about the significance of what you just learned. Now that you know how to display any image on your computer screen and link any part of it to any object on your computer, you can make your computer do anything you want it to do for your presentations.

Chapter 19

Text Files

In addition to making text slides in the BUL format, PODIUM also provides a TEX format. You enter the text exactly the same way for a TEX as a BUL file; the only difference is that when you save the file, you give it a .TEX instead of a .BUL file extension.

When PODIUM displays TEX files, it always left justifies the text on your screen. Up to ten lines of text fit on the screen. If there are more than ten lines, PODIUM activates the PageUp and PageDown keys to let you page through the text. Windows and OS/2 users can also use double clicks to page up and down; double-clicking the left mouse button pages down, and double-clicking the right button pages up.

Using Columns in Text Files

During a presentation there are times when you want to display two columns of text so you can compare what is in column one with column two during your talk. To signal the beginning of a column, PODIUM uses a special character called the "pipe," which is the | key on your computer. The next slide you create, "Old Learning Versus New Learning," will give you practice using the | key to make columns.

Old Learning Versus New Learning

The "Old Learning Versus New Learning" file is called LEARNING.TEX and appears in Figure 19.1. Notice how it uses the | character to indicate where column two will begin. Type the LEARNING.TEX file with your text editor, and save it in your TQM directory.

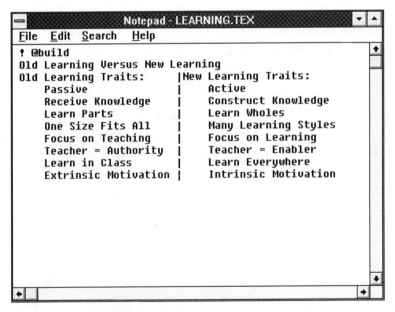

FIGURE 19.1
The "Old Learning Versus New Learning" file
LEARNING.TEX.

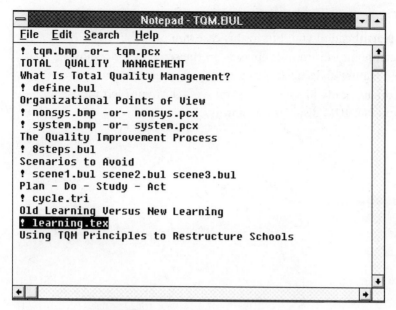

FIGURE 19.2
Linking LEARNING.TEX to the TQM.BUL home file.

Linking the Learning Text to Old Learning Versus New Learning

To link the LEARNING.TEX file to your TQM presentation, edit the
file TQM.BUL, inserting the line highlighted in Figure 19.2. Save
the TQM.BUL file and return to PODIUM. Now click on the bullet
for "Old Learning Versus New Learning," and the LEARNING.TEX
slide will begin to appear. Because the @build option is on, you
must click your left mouse button to reveal each line of the slide. If
you want it all to appear at once, remove the @build option. Windows and OS/2 users can do this by pulling down the Effects menu
and deselecting Build; DOS users must remove it by editing the
LEARNING.TEX file.

You will probably prefer the @build option in this case, because
otherwise too much information appears on the screen at once,

and your audience may become confused. Sometimes it is good to let them read ahead of you, but in this case you probably wish to discuss each point in turn as it appears on the screen. Notice how the @build feature gives perfect timing to your presentation; as soon as you are ready for the next point, you click your left mouse button, and PODIUM displays it instantly.

Chapter 20

Building with Clustered Bullets

The build feature can also be used on any bullet slide, whether or not the cluster feature is also on. To illustrate this, we will create a slide explaining how to use TQM principles to restructure schools.

Using TQM Principles to Restructure Schools

Figure 20.1 shows the text of the SCHOOLS.BUL file. Use your text editor to create it, and save the SCHOOLS.BUL file in your TQM directory.

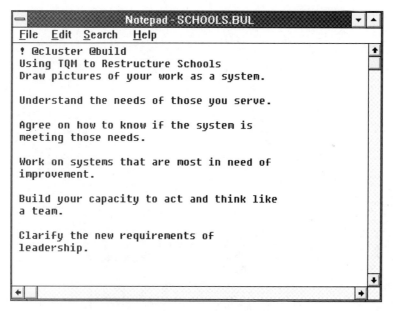

FIGURE 20.1
The SCHOOLS.BUL restructuring file.

Linking the Schools Restructuring File

To link the SCHOOLS.BUL file to your TQM presentation, edit the
file TQM.BUL, inserting the line highlighted in Figure 20.2. Save
the TQM.BUL file, and return to PODIUM. Now click on the bullet
for "Using TQM Principles to Restructure Schools"; the
SCHOOLS.BUL slide will begin to appear. Because the @build
option is on, you must click your left mouse button to reveal each
cluster in the slide.

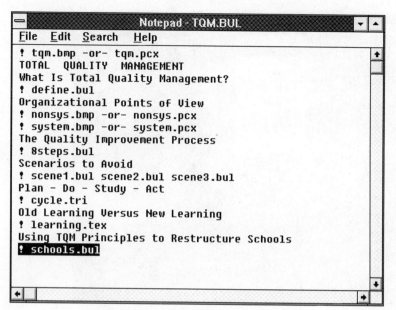

FIGURE 20.2
Linking SCHOOLS.BUL to schools restructuring.

How Clusters Interact with Builds

Notice how the cluster feature interacts with the build feature. Normally the build feature causes one more line of your slide to appear, but when the cluster feature is also turned on, each left mouse click makes an entire cluster appear.

You may wish to experiment with how the cluster and build features interact by turning them on and off one by one. DOS users must edit their presentation files manually to turn these features on and off. Windows and OS/2 users can use the Effects menu; when you choose or deselect a feature with the Effects menu, PODIUM automatically updates your presentation file for you,

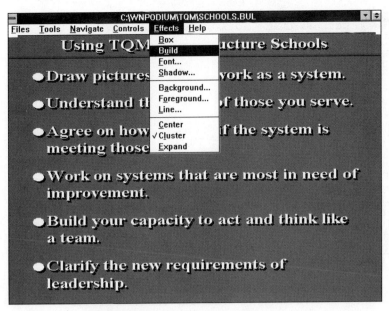

FIGURE 20.3
How the Effects menu appears when PODIUM displays a
bullet file.

making the edit you would ordinarily need to type by hand. Figure
20.3 shows how the Effects menu appears when you pull it down
while PODIUM is displaying a bullet file; this menu makes it very
easy to use PODIUM special effects.

Chapter 21

Digital Chalk

Perhaps you have already tried PODIUM's digital chalk feature; if not, you should try it now. The paragraphs ahead show how to activate the chalk, erase it, and change its color.

Activating Chalk with Your Mouse

With digital chalk you can write down ideas or emphasize existing points directly on-screen during your presentations. Whenever you want to use the chalk, simply press and hold down both mouse buttons at the same time; the mouse cursor becomes a piece of chalk. As you move the mouse with both buttons down, the chalk will draw on your screen. You can draw over any text slide or image PODIUM displays. You can even draw on motion video sequences while they are playing. For example, Figure 21.1 shows how digital chalk was used to draw the escape path of the news correspondent reporting on the Tacoma Narrows Bridge when it collapsed.

FIGURE 21.1
Using PODIUM's digital chalk to show the escape route of a news correspondent when the Tacoma Narrows Bridge collapsed. Used by permission of Wiley Education Software, publisher of the Tacoma Narrows videodisc.

Erasing Chalk

To erase the digital chalkboard, release the mouse buttons and press E (for erase). PODIUM will redraw the screen exactly as it appeared before you began writing on it with the chalk.

Changing the Color of Chalk

To change the color of the chalk, press C (for color) while writing
with the chalk and holding both mouse buttons down. Each time
you press C, PODIUM will change the chalk to the next color.
Holding the C down will cause PODIUM to cycle through all 16
chalk colors, one after the other, letting you write with a rainbow.

Chapter 22

Compact Disc Audio

All three versions of PODIUM support compact disc audio, and they work with any audio CD you purchase from an audio store.

Selecting a CD for Your Presentation

Music works like magic. It is amazing how a little music triggered by a slide enhances its effect. You can use music to create a mood, add excitement, evoke empathy, or simply entertain. With PODIUM, CD audio clips can be triggered by any bullet or line of hypertext. Any trigger you place on a hyperpicture with a trigger file can be linked to compact disc audio. CD audio clips can also trigger objects timed to appear in synchronization with the music.

Using compact discs does have a limitation: Unless all of the CD audio you plan to use resides on the same CD, you have to switch discs during your presentation. Although you can work within the limits of a single CD because compact discs contain so much music, you still may want to take clips from more than one CD. To avoid disc switching, digitize the clips with an audio digitizer and play them back from your hard disk as waveform audio files. Chapter 24, Digital Audio, shows how to do that.

CD Audio Clipmaking

All three versions of PODIUM provide a compact disc audio clip-maker. In the Windows and OS/2 versions, you access this tool from the PODIUM Tools menu. DOS users access it by pressing F5 and clicking on the Compact Disc button. Figure 22.1 shows PODIUM's compact disc Clipmaker.

Use PODIUM to get the CD Audio tool on your computer screen now. Notice the Play and Pause buttons, and a starting and ending location for your clip. The starting and ending locations are in red book format, consisting of minute, second, and frame. For example, the red book address 22.13.40 refers to the location 22 minutes, 13 seconds, and 40 frames from the beginning of the CD. Compact discs have 75 frames per second.

Try clicking on the CD Audio controls. Put in different start and stop locations, and click the Start button to rehearse the clip. To stop the audio, click Stop or Pause. To resume play, click Pause again; it is a toggle. Whenever the Pause button is on, PODIUM will display (in the upper left corner) the number of the frame the compact disc is on.

Audio CDs are organized into tracks, with one song residing on each track. The PODIUM Track buttons let you access the CD by track. When you click on the Track buttons, PODIUM updates the Clip Start and Clip Stop numbers to show you the precise frame location of the track.

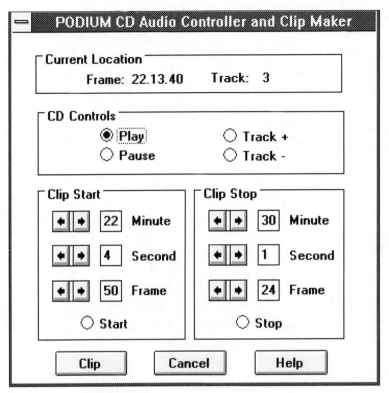

FIGURE 22.1
PODIUM for Windows CD Audio Controller and Clipmaker.
Used by permission of the University of Delaware.

When you find the clip you want with the CD Audio tool, Windows and OS/2 users can click on the Clip button to copy it to the clipboard from which it can be pasted into a presentation file with your text editor. DOS users must edit their presentation file manually.

For example, suppose you want to link a compact disc audio clip that will play music to accompany the definition of TQM. Assuming the clip starts at location 6.47.21 and ends at 7.5.64, Figure 22.2 shows the line to insert in your TQM.BUL file.

When you save the TQM.BUL file and click on the bullet titled "What Is Total Quality Management," you will hear the CD audio clip as the definition appears on the screen.

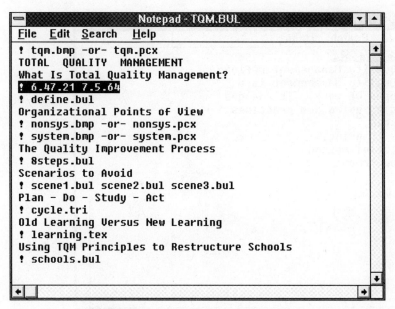

FIGURE 22.2
Linking CD audio background music to the "What Is Total
Quality Management" bullet.

Think about how the object-oriented approach applies to the way
you linked the CD audio clip. Because you put the CD clip in the
TQM.BUL file right before the link to DEFINE.BUL, PODIUM plays
the audio and then launches DEFINE.BUL. If you wanted to
launch the DEFINE.BUL file somewhere else with different audio
in it, you could do so by entering a different clip address. But suppose you always want DEFINE.BUL to have that sound track.
Instead of entering it each time you link DEFINE.BUL, you can
make it part of the DEFINE.BUL file by typing it at the very top of
DEFINE.BUL, as shown in Figure 22.3.

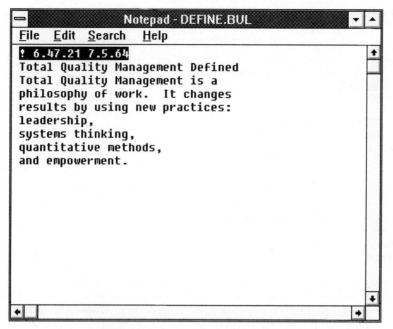

FIGURE 22.3
Making the TQM definition always trigger the same CD audio clip.

CD Audio Special Effects

There is a wide range of special effects you can achieve with compact disc audio. Figures 22.4 and 22.5 provide a few examples; they are bullet files in which each bullet describes the effect it launches. Notice the use of @wait=KEY and @wait=END in these examples. In PODIUM, compact disc audio is asynchronous, meaning that once it starts playing, PODIUM immediately moves to your next multimedia object. @wait=KEY makes PODIUM await a keypress before moving on. @wait=END makes PODIUM wait until the audio ends.

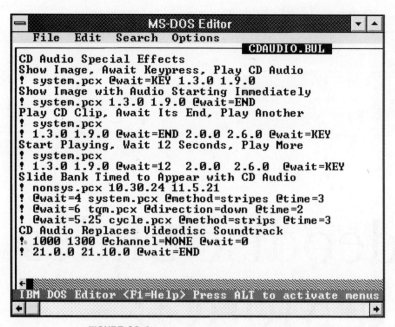

FIGURE 22.4
Compact disc audio special effects (DOS users).

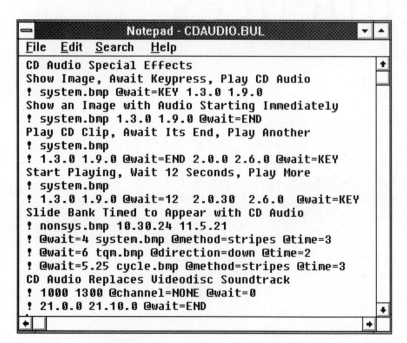

FIGURE 22.5
Compact disc audio special effects (Windows and OS/2 users).

Chapter 23

Videodisc Slides and Motion Sequences

All three versions of PODIUM support videodisc, and they work with any CAV videodisc. Thousands of CAV discs already pressed for use in education and training are cataloged in *The Videodisc Compendium* (1993). You can also have custom videodiscs pressed with your own video on them for as little as $300; Part 3 of this book tells how.

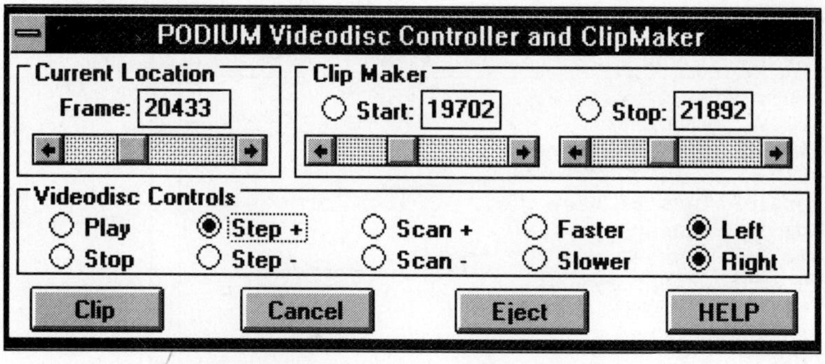

FIGURE 23.1
PODIUM for Windows Videodisc Controller and Clipmaker.
Used by permission of the University of Delaware.

Videodisc Clipmaking

All three versions of PODIUM come with a videodisc clipmaker. In the Windows and OS/2 versions, you access this tool from the PODIUM Tools menu. DOS users access it by pressing F5 and clicking on the Videodisc button. Figure 23.1 shows the PODIUM Videodisc Controller and Clipmaker.

Use PODIUM to get the Videodisc tool on your computer screen now. Notice how there are buttons you use to play and stop your videodisc, step forward and backward one frame at a time, and scan forward or backward at different speeds. Whenever the videodisc is paused, PODIUM will show which frame you are on in the upper left corner of the tool. Each CAV videodisc can contain up to 54,000 frames per side. The frames are numbered from 1 through 54000. PODIUM recognizes numbers in this range as videodisc frame numbers. When you play a videodisc at normal speed, it plays back 30 frames per second; thus, each side of a videodisc can hold up to 30 minutes of full-motion video, including a stereo sound track.

By browsing the videodisc, you decide on the start and stop locations for your clip, which you enter in the start and stop fields. Pressing the Start button lets you rehearse your clip to be sure you

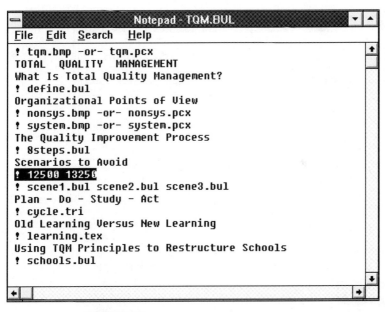

FIGURE 23.2

Linking a videodisc motion sequence to the scenarios to avoid.

got it right. When you find the clip you want, Windows and OS/2 users can click on the Clip button to copy it to the clipboard from which it can be pasted into the presentation file with the text editor. DOS users must edit their presentation files manually.

For example, suppose you want to link a videodisc clip that presages the three scenarios to avoid in your TQM presentation. Assuming the clip starts at location 12500 and ends at 13250, Figure 23.2 shows the line to insert in the TQM.BUL file.

When you save the TQM.BUL file and click on the bullet titled "Scenarios to Avoid," you see how the videodisc motion sequence plays and then waits for you to click your left mouse button to move on to the first scenario. If you do not have a videodisc player attached, PODIUM will tell you what frames it would play if you had one.

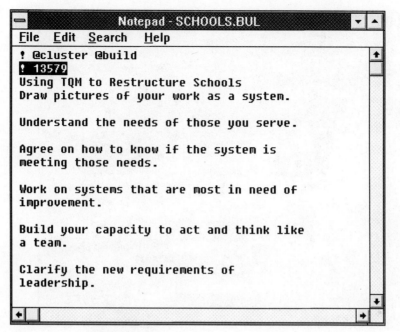

FIGURE 23.3
Making a videodisc image underlay the bullets in
SCHOOLS.BUL.

Using Videodisc Slides as Backdrops

It is easy to underlay any PODIUM presentation file with a
videodisc image. Any bitmap or videodisc image linked before the
heading of a file will appear as a backdrop to that file. For example,
suppose you want to make frame 13579 underlay the bullets in
your SCHOOLS.BUL file. Figure 23.3 shows how to insert a link to
that frame number prior to the heading of the bullets; Figure 23.4
shows how it will appear during the presentation.

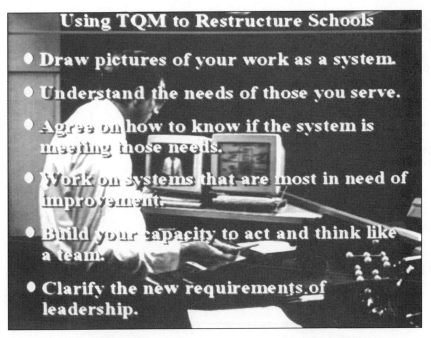

FIGURE 23.4
The videodisc image underlays the SCHOOLS.BUL bullets.

Videodisc Special Effects

You can make many special effects with videodisc slides and motion sequences. Figure 23.5 provides a few examples; it is a bullet file in which each bullet describes the effect it launches. The source and target effects make PODIUM adjust the frame of the videodisc and the size of the displayed frame. Only PODIUM for DOS and PODIUM for Windows will respond to source and target effects. Because of the DVI architecture used in PODIUM for Presentation Manager, it can display videodisc images in full size only.

Videodisc motion sequences are asynchronous; that is, their timing does not depend on the timing of any other events. When you use @wait= after a motion sequence, PODIUM will begin counting time from the beginning of the motion. If the wait is longer than the motion sequence, PODIUM will hold the last frame of the

```
Videodisc Special Effects
Search a Frame, Wait for a Key, Search Another
! 3333 @wait=key 4444
This does the same with a period
! 3333 . 4444
Play Part of the Video Frame in a Window
! 1000 1100 @source=20,20,40,40  @target=50,50,70,70
Play All of the Video Frame in a Window
! 1000 1100 @source=0,0,100,100  @target=10,10,20,20
Play the Right Channel Only
! 1000 1100 @channel=B
Play with No Sound
! 1000 1100 @channel=none
Play at slow speed
! 1000 1100 @speed=25
Play at lightning speed
! 1000 1100 @speed=300
Search frame 2222, Wait 4, Play from 100 to 500
! 2222 @wait=4  100 500
Show Four Frames as Fast as Possible
!100 @wait=0 200 @wait=0 300 @wait=0 400
Motion, wait 4, Motion
! 100 200 @wait=4 500 600
Motion, Motion
!100 200 500 600
Motion, Motion, Slide
!100 200 500 600 700
Motion, Slide, Motion
!100 200 500 . 600 700
Slide Bank
!100 . 200 . 500 . 600 . 700
Cut a Videodisc Slide Into a Bitmap
! system.pcx -or- system.bmp
! @under 1000 @target=30,30,70,70
Still Video Showing Through a VGA Graphic
! udcrest.pcx -or- udcrest.bmp @under 1000
```

FIGURE 23.5
Videodisc special effects.

motion sequence on the screen until the wait time has elapsed. If
the wait is shorter, PODIUM will move to the next object when the
time passes. If the @wait= is followed by the word end, PODIUM
will wait for the end of the motion sequence and then continue.

Chapter 24

Digital Audio

T he most flexible way to add audio to your multimedia presentations is to use a waveform digital audio device. With audio digitizers you can record any sound from any source and then have instant access to it. You can record the audio you wish to accompany a slide and easily link it to your presentation.

Digitizing Audio

PODIUM for DOS does not support digital audio; DOS users who want digital audio have a very good reason to upgrade to Windows, which supports a wide range of digital audio boards.

PODIUM for Windows contains the comprehensive waveform audio recording and clipmaking tool shown in Figure 24.1. You access this tool from the PODIUM Tools menu. PODIUM for Windows saves audio files with a .WAV file extension. In addition to playing back WAV files that you record with PODIUM, PODIUM

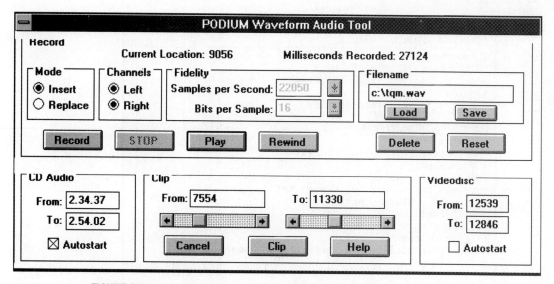

FIGURE 24.1
PODIUM for Windows digital audio recording and clipmaking tool.
Used by permission of the University of Delaware.

for Windows can also play back any WAV file that you create with
any other Windows waveform audio program.

PODIUM for Presentation Manager uses the audio digitizing capability of the ActionMedia II adapter. By recording both video and
audio files from the same adapter, it saves a slot in your computer.
PODIUM for Presentation Manager comes with a comprehensive
tool for digitizing audio; to see it, pull down the Tools menu and
select DVI Audio Capture.

Linking Digitized Audio

To link a waveform audio file to one of your presentation items,
type its filename in the place you want to link it. For example, the
CD-ROM that came with this book includes a digital audio clip that
explains the two organizational bitmaps in the TQM presentation.

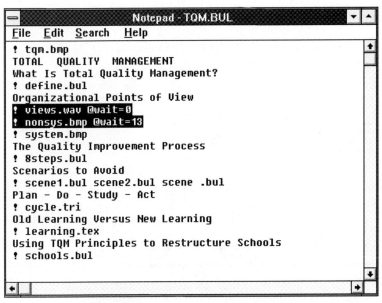

FIGURE 24.2

Linking waveform audio to TQM organizational bitmaps (Windows users).

If you are using PODIUM for Windows and have a waveform audio driver loaded, copy the files from the WAVAUDIO directory of the CD-ROM to your TQM directory. For example, if your CD-ROM is drive D, and you installed PODIUM on drive C, type the following:

        copy d:\wavaudio*.* c:\tqm

If you are using PODIUM for Presentation Manager and have the ActionMedia II device driver installed, copy the files from the AVSAUDIO directory of the CD-ROM to your TQM directory. For example, if your CD-ROM is drive D, and you installed PODIUM on drive C, type the following:

        copy d:\avsaudio*.* c:\tqm

Figures 24.2 and 24.3 show how to link and how to time the TQM digital audio clip with the two organizational bitmaps. When you click on the bullet titled "Organizational Points of View" during your presentation, the slides will appear with audio commentary.

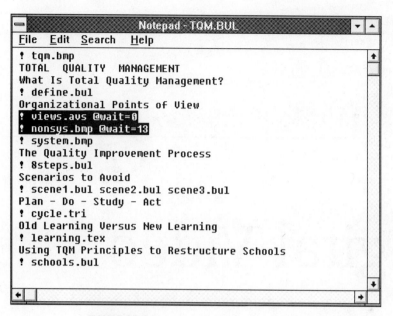

FIGURE 24.3
Linking waveform audio to TQM organizational bitmaps (OS/2 users).

The background music was generated by the *Band-in-a-Box* program that is described in Part Three of this book; the narrator's voice is that of the author.

Chapter 25

Digital Video

Digital video is the hottest buzzword in multimedia. By making it possible to store motion video on your hard drive and play it back without requiring external devices like videodisc players, digital video makes multimedia portable. To play back digital video with high quality, however, hardware assistance in the form of a digital video board is required. If your computer does not have digital video hardware, its microprocessor will be given the task of playing back the video. It will not be able to play it full-screen at 30 frames per second, which is the speed of videotapes and discs.

Digitizing Video

To digitize video you need a digital video capture adapter. The type of adapter depends on the version of PODIUM you choose.

PODIUM for DOS cannot play back digital video. If you are a DOS user and you want to use digital video, you should consider

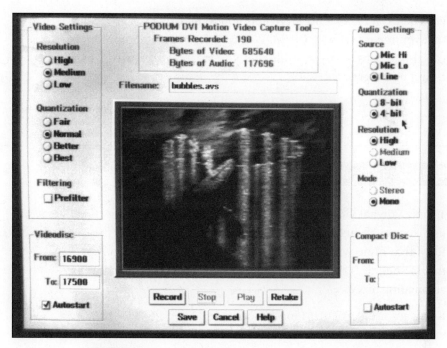

FIGURE 25.1
The digital video recording tool in PODIUM for Presentation Manager. Used by permission of the University of Delaware.

upgrading to Windows or OS/2 so you can use the tools described in the next paragraphs.

PODIUM for Windows plays *Video for Windows* AVI files and Action-Media II AVS files. You can capture video for PODIUM with any digital video board for which there is a Windows MCI device driver. For example, the Creative Labs Video Blaster, the New Media Graphics Super VideoWindows, and the IBM/Intel ActionMedia II board work well with PODIUM.

PODIUM for Presentation Manager plays DVI files on the Action-Media II adapter, which is available in Micro Channel and industry standard AT bus versions. PODIUM for Presentation Manager contains the comprehensive DVI motion-recording and clipmaking tool shown in Figure 25.1. You access this tool from the PODIUM Tools menu. PODIUM for Presentation Manager saves video files with an .AVS file extension. In addition to playing back AVS files that you record with PODIUM, PODIUM for Presentation Manager can also play back any AVS file that you create with any other DVI recording program.

Linking Digitized Video

To link a digital video file to one of your presentation items, type its filename in the place you want to link it. For example, the CD-ROM that came with this book includes three digital video clips that (1) define TQM, (2) discuss its benefits, and (3) describe it as an ongoing process.

If you are using PODIUM for Windows and have *Video for Windows* installed on your computer *without* an Indeo driver, copy the files from the AVIVIDEO directory of the CD-ROM to your TQM directory. For example, if your CD-ROM is drive D, and you installed PODIUM on drive C, type the following:

```
copy  d:\avivideo\*.*  c:\tqm
```

If you are using PODIUM for Windows and have *Video for Windows* installed on your computer *with* an Indeo driver, copy the files from the INDEO directory of the CD-ROM to your TQM directory. For example, if your CD-ROM is drive D, and you installed PODIUM on drive C, type the following:

```
copy  d:\indeo\*.*  c:\tqm
```

If you are using PODIUM for Windows or PODIUM for Presentation Manager and have the ActionMedia II device driver installed, copy the files from the AVSVIDEO directory of the CD-ROM to your TQM directory. For example, if your CD-ROM is drive D, and you installed PODIUM on drive C, type the following:

```
copy  d:\avsvideo\*.*  c:\tqm
```

Figure 25.2 shows how *Video for Windows* users link the three clips to the definition of TQM. Likewise, Figure 25.3 shows how Action-Media II users make the linkages.

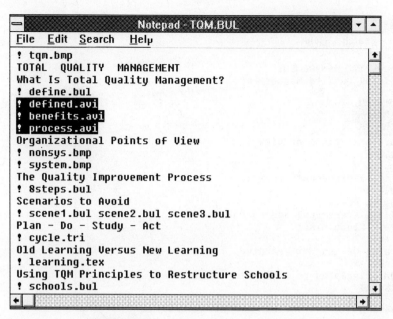

FIGURE 25.2

How *Video for Windows* users link digital video to the definition of TQM.

While running your TQM PODIUM presentation, click on the bullet titled "What Is Total Quality Management" to reveal the definition of TQM. Clicking again will trigger a digital video clip showing the world-renowned TQM clinician Verne Harnish defining Total Quality Management. When that clip ends, a left mouse click will take you to a testimonial of the benefits of TQM delivered by John Sample, President of Business Interiors Inc. Your next left mouse click will advance you to Miller Business Systems' Vice President Stan Feldman, who tells how TQM is an ongoing process. These three clips are taken from an excellent three-volume TQM video workshop by Verne Harnish. The author is grateful to Mr. Harnish for granting permission to include these clips. For more information about ordering the videotapes, contact

CareerTrack Publications
3085 Center Green Drive
Boulder, CO 80301

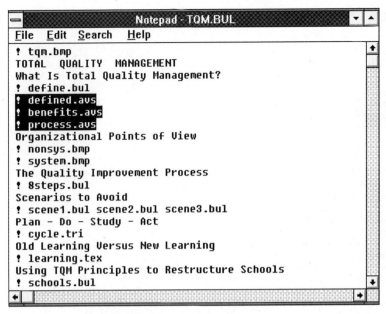

FIGURE 25.3
How ActionMedia II users link digital video to the definition of TQM.

or phone (303) 440-7440. To schedule Verne Harnish for a private workshop, keynote, or special presentation, phone (800) 325-5854.

Live Video Feeds

Suppose late-breaking news applies to your TQM presentation. For example, imagine that world leaders have assembled to decide what is the greatest obstacle to reducing nuclear arms, preventing terrorism, or solving the world hunger problem, and the news channels are broadcasting live coverage. If you have a live video feed connected to your video overlay or digital video card, you can switch to it instantly with PODIUM whenever you want it on your presentation screen. You can even draw with PODIUM's digital chalk to annotate the live video feed.

Dos Users

PODIUM for DOS supports the M-Motion card on the Micro Channel and the School Board on the industry standard AT bus. These cards have three video inputs, and PODIUM supports them all. To show feed one, press ALT-1; feed two is ALT-2; and feed three is ALT-3. You can even link a live video feed to a presentation item with the @vinput special effect. Simply link @vinput=1 for feed one, @vinput=2 for feed two, or @vinput=3 for feed three. For example, if you want a live video feed from input two to appear on your screen when you select the item "Live Video on Location," you would type the following into your presentation file:

```
Live Video on Location
! @vinput=2
```

If you have a videodisc player controlled by PODIUM, it must always be connected to video feed one; connect your other video sources to inputs two and three on your video overlay card.

Windows Users

PODIUM for Windows supports every overlay card for which there is an MCI device driver. PODIUM for Windows will support up to three video inputs. To show feed one, press ALT-1; feed two is ALT-2; and feed three is ALT-3. These feeds are also available anytime from the PODIUM Controls menu.

You can even link a live video feed to a presentation item with the @vinput special effect. Link @vinput=1 for feed one, @vinput=2 for feed two, or @vinput=3 for feed three. For example, if you want a live video feed from input two to appear on your screen when you select the item "Live Video on Location," you would type the following into your presentation file:

```
Live Video on Location
! @vinput=2
```

If you have a videodisc player controlled by PODIUM, it must always be connected to video feed one; connect your other video sources to inputs two and three on your video overlay card.

OS/2 Users

PODIUM for Presentation Manager supports live video feeds from the ActionMedia II DVI board. Press ALT-V to show a live video feed; this option is also available anytime from the PODIUM Controls menu.

You can even link a live video feed to a presentation item with the @vinput special effect. Simply link @vinput to the item. For example, if you want a live video feed to appear on your screen when you select the item "Live Video on Location," you would type the following into your presentation file:

Live Video on Location
! @vinput

The ActionMedia II board has only one video input. If you have multiple sources to connect, you will need a video switcher. Radio Shack sells one (catalog number 15-1956A) that does the job nicely for less than $20. You can connect up to four video inputs with stereo sound, and simply press a button to select the feed you want.

Chapter 26

Applications as Objects

In addition to all of the multimedia objects PODIUM recognizes, you can also link any application on your computer via PODIUM's OS special effect. OS stands for operating system. You use it to make your computer start other programs that return to your PODIUM presentation when they complete.

Due to the memory limitations of DOS, this feature is not very practical for DOS users; unless the application you link is small, there will not be enough memory to run it. Because Windows and OS/2 use virtual memory, Windows and OS/2 users can link any application on their computers to their PODIUM presentation items.

Lotus 1-2-3 Graphs of Corporate Data

PODIUM can launch *Lotus 1-2-3* and tell it which spreadsheet to graph. When you trigger an item linked to *Lotus 1-2-3*, PODIUM will start *Lotus 1-2-3* and make it plot the graph. This is a real-time plot; that is, PODIUM tells *Lotus 1-2-3* to plot the current version of your spreadsheet, reflecting any last minute changes that may have occurred in your data.

For example, to make *Lotus 1-2-3* plot the current graph of PODIUM sales, you would make the following link:

> PODIUM Sales Activity
> ! @os=c:\123g\123g.exe podrep.gph

After you view the graph and close *Lotus 1-2-3*, PODIUM returns you to the point in your presentation at which you launched the spreadsheet.

Database Reports of Product Information

You can use the OS feature to launch any report-generating software to produce an up-to-the-minute report on-screen. For example, with PODIUM for Windows you can link any presentation item to Microsoft *Access*, give it the name of the database you want to open, and execute a macro to make *Access* display the report you want. To get a list of users who have purchased PODIUM for DOS, you would make a link as follows:

Who Uses PODIUM for DOS?
! @os=c:\access\msaccess.exe podium.mdb/excl/x customer dataset

Word-processed Documents

The OS feature can be used to launch word-processed documents. For example, to launch a *WordPerfect* document called SYLLABUS.DOC, you would type the following:

```
Course Outline for Art 101
! @os=c:\wp51\wp.exe  c:\art101\syllabus.doc
```

ToolBook Books and PowerPoint Presentations

PODIUM for Windows handles *ToolBook* books and *PowerPoint* presentations as objects. That means if you link an object with a .TBK file extension, PODIUM will launch it as a *ToolBook* book. Similarly, if you link an object with a .PPT file extension, PODIUM will launch the *PowerPoint* presentation. When you finish, PODIUM will return to the point at which you launched the *ToolBook* book or *PowerPoint* presentation. Here is how easy it is to make links to *ToolBook* books and *PowerPoint* presentations:

```
Mozart's G Major Piano Concerto
! K453.tbk
The Bottom Line
! finance.ppt
```

Extending PODIUM

In addition to linking applications that others have written, you can also use the OS feature to link any program you write in any programming language. Thus, if there is a feature PODIUM does not have that you would like to use, you can write your own code in any programming language and link the resulting EXE file into the place in your presentation file where you want to use it.

This concludes the PODIUM tutorial. Having learned how to flow any text and any picture onto the screen and link any part of them to any other object on your computer, you are now empowered to create effective multimedia presentations. The next step is to learn how to implement them, which is the subject of the last part of this book.

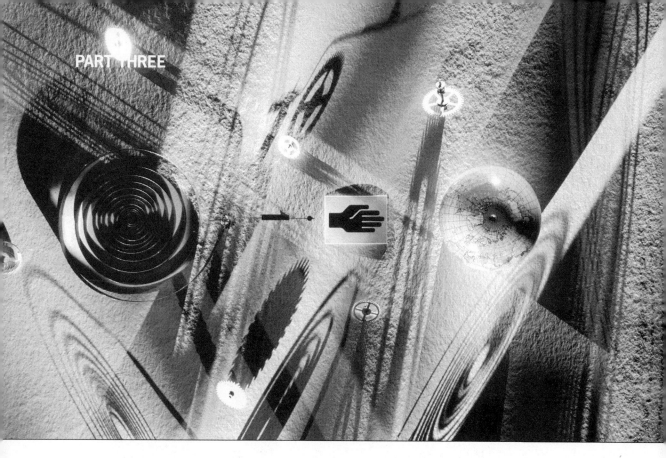

PART THREE

Multimedia is challenging to implement. You must think through what you want to present, how you will create it, where you will deliver it, what equipment you will need, and how you will get it there. If you plan to equip existing facilities for multimedia, you will have to work with limitations imposed by buildings constructed without multimedia in mind. If you are constructing new facilities, you will want to be sure that you do not forget something important when designing them. Making multimedia portable so you can take your presentations on the road imposes yet another set of needs and constraints, both on you and on your choice of a site for the presentation.

This implementation guide is designed to help you think through the process, to avoid purchasing things you do not need, to make wise decisions procuring and installing multimedia devices, and to make sure you will have everything you need. If you are building new facilities, the section on planning new construction provides

Implementation

you with an outline of items you should review with your architect. Because it is more common to retrofit existing facilities, this guide also shows how to make the best of renovation projects and how to set priorities that fit within your budget.

One of the most exciting aspects of multimedia is how portable it is becoming. The portability section advises you on selecting hardware that is easy to set up and minimizes your dependency on your host to supply local equipment. Checklists are provided for you to make sure you do not forget something important when you travel with your setup and to prevent your host from forgetting something you cannot bring with you.

Chapter 27

Multimedia Creation Station

The term "creation station" refers to the multimedia equipment used to create your presentation. Schools and businesses usually set up a creation station in their audiovisual media centers, where it serves all their employees. Media support staff trained in using a creation station digitize images and sound tracks for the presenters, who can use any word processor to link them into PODIUM presentations.

If you do not have an organization large enough to justify a central media support unit, you might consider locating your creation station in your office. Some teachers and executives prefer to do their own creating on their own time at home; Figure 27.1 shows an example of a creation station in a home office.

Either way, you need to understand what a creation station is and how to put one together. Accordingly, this guide begins by identifying and explaining creation station concepts, providing checklists

FIGURE 27.1
The author seated at his home creation station.

that show what equipment you will need, and making recommendations for creation station software.

Concepts

The creation station consists of a computer and peripheral devices used to create multimedia objects or import them into your presentation. Many creation station tasks are computer-intensive. To avoid wasting precious time waiting for objects to be processed, the computer in your creation station should have a fast microprocessor configured to complete its tasks quickly.

If you plan to enter a lot of text from books, manuals, charts, magazines, or other printed materials, a scanner can save lots of time. The new lower-cost flatbed and hand-held scanners have expanded features and accuracy. Most of the text in the TQM presentation in Part Two of this book was hand scanned from articles about TQM.

In addition to scanning text, scanners can also produce bitmapped images for display in your presentations. Color scanners input pictures in color. Color scanning is computer-intensive; you will definitely want a fast processor if you plan to do much color work.

An increasingly large percentage of information is transmitted through video. Television broadcasts, videotapes, and videodiscs provide a rich store of images, audio, and video that can be used in your presentations. Moreover, any object you want to input that has not already been photographed or taped can be converted into a video signal by shooting it with a camera or camcorder. To make use of this wide array of video source material, your creation station should contain a video digitizing board.

If you have a video digitizer and you work with 35-mm slides, you will also want your creation station to have a slide-to-video converter. With a slide-to-video converter you can use any 35-mm camera to take your slides, and then you can digitize them at your creation station. Many practitioners use digital cameras that digitize and save pictures as bitmaps instead of shooting 35-mm film. This avoids waiting for the film to be developed, but what will happen when computer screens and projectors increase resolution higher than your old bitmaps? If you did not use film, you will not be able to redigitize your slides at the higher resolution; instead, you will have to redo your photography, assuming the objects or scenes you shot are still available.

Just as digital video boards can capture any picture, waveform audio boards can digitize any sound, which can be input from a record, tape, compact disc, microphone, or any other audio source. Your creation station should have such an audio-digitizing capability and the audio equipment needed to play audio into it and play back the resulting digital waveform file.

It is common for multimedia computers to have built-in CD-ROM players. In addition to being used for data, most CD-ROM players can also play audio from any commercial audio CD. Your creation station should have a CD-ROM player that can play audio CDs.

MIDI is another option you may want to include in your creation station. If you do not know how to use a MIDI sequencer to arrange your own music, there are commercial clip libraries of MIDI music sequences that work like clip art for pictures. Once you purchase a MIDI clip library, you have the right to use any MIDI clip in it as background music for your presentations. Check the license carefully to see if any restrictions apply. For example, some clip providers require that you pay an additional fee if you distribute your presentation to others.

Recommendations

Table 27.1 contains a checklist of items to consider for your creation station. To learn about newer models, you should refer to Chapter 32 of this book, Catalogs and Buyers' Guides, or contact the author for an updated checklist.

Bitmap Editors and Converters

With more than 30 graphics standards already defined by the computer industry, there are dozens of graphics editors available. While it is beyond the scope of this book to describe them all, recommendations are provided that should help you select graphics software for your creation station.

Microsoft Windows comes with *Paintbrush*, a program that is good for users on a budget because it does not cost extra. Figure 27.2

TABLE 27.1 Recommended Creation Station Hardware

Computer

☐	Processor	486 processor preferred; speed is important
☐	Memory	8 megabyte RAM preferred; 4 meg minimum
☐	Hard Disk	400 megabytes preferred; 60 megabyte minimum
☐	Mouse	Microsoft Mouse feels best
☐	Monitor	Color VGA, SVGA, or XGA monitor
☐	Backup	Means of backing up hard disk to tape, optical read/write disks, or cartridges; Bernoulli 150 recommended

Audio

☐	Headphones	Stereo headphones provide a private means of listening to audio
☐	Amplifier	Stereo amplifier unless your speakers are self-powered
☐	Speaker	Yamaha MS-202 is a nice self-powered speaker for multimedia
☐	CD Player	Audio compact disc player for playing CDs
☐	Tape	Audiocassette deck for playing audio tapes
☐	Turntable	Only if you need to play records
☐	Mixer	Eight-in, two-out audio mixer
☐	Digitizer	Digital audio board compatible with Microsoft MCI
☐	MIDI	MIDI adapter with MIDI keyboard or MIDI sound module

Digital Video

☐	Adapter	Digital video board compatible with Microsoft MCI
☐	Camcorder	Camcorder provides camera and video recording (Hi8 format recommended)
☐	Slide-to-Video	Slide-to-Video converter for digitizing slides; RasterOps Expresso recommended
☐	Copy stand	Copy stand with lights (for lighting artwork or other physical objects)
☐	Monitor	Video monitor for previewing tapes and positioning images

Analog Video

☐	Adapter	Video overlay board compatible with Microsoft MCI
☐	Videodisc	Videodisc player compatible with Microsoft MCI
☐	VCR	S-VHS format for playing back VHS and S-VHS videotapes

Scanners

☐	Flatbed	For scanning documents and flat art
☐	Hand-Held	Portable scanner that can travel with you
☐	OCR	Make sure your scanner comes with software that has optical character recognition (OCR) for scanning text into documents

Cables and Adapters

☐	Cables	For connecting all of the above
☐	Adapters	To make the cables fit the connectors on your multimedia circuit boards and peripherals

FIGURE 27.2
Microsoft Windows *Paintbrush* provides drawing and bitmap editing tools. Used by permission of Microsoft Corporation.

shows how it provides a palette of drawing and editing tools that let you create bitmaps and cut and paste them. A color palette lets you choose and change colors. For example, if you have a picture in which you want to change all the green pixels to blue, a couple of mouse clicks will recolor them. You can even convert PCX images to BMP and vice versa. However, *Paintbrush* does not include special effects like gradients, blending, slanting, aligning, and flowing text along a curve.

Micrografx's *Graphics Works* is a graphics package that overcomes this limitation. Figure 27.3 shows how it provides a complete suite of drawing, charting, graphing, and photo-editing programs. *Graphics Works* can import TIFF, PCX, GIF, and TGA images and

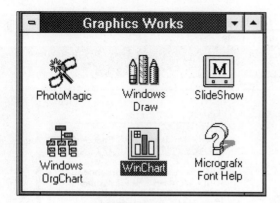

FIGURE 27.3
Programs bundled in Micrografx's *Graphics Works* package. Used by permission of Micrografx.

convert them to the BMP format used by PODIUM and most other Windows programs. The package is relatively low-cost and provides most of the tools you will need.

Bitmaps can be compressed using a technique called run-length encoding (RLE). When this book went to press, most graphics packages were not yet supporting RLE files. As Figure 27.4 shows, a shareware program called *Paint Shop Pro* does. If you read an image into *Paint Shop Pro* and choose the RLE feature to compress it, you will be pleasantly surprised by how much disk space you save. For example, the bitmaps used in the TQM tutorial in Part Two of this book occupied 180K of space each before they were RLE compressed with *Paint Shop Pro*; after compression the bitmaps averaged 25K each.

Kodak's Photo CD

For presenters who do not have their own digitizing equipment, Kodak's Photo CD may provide a cost-effective way of taking pic-

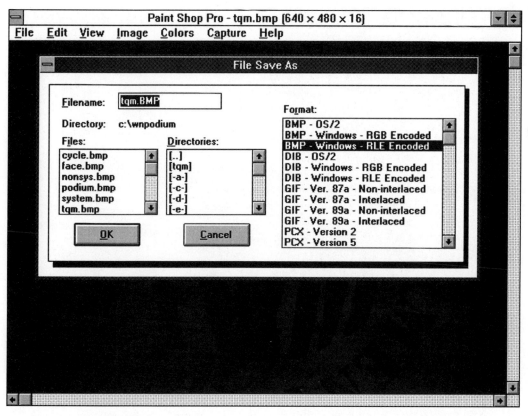

FIGURE 27.4
Paint Shop Pro can compress bitmaps. Used by permission of JASC, Inc.

tures for use in presentations. You take your negatives or film to a nearby photofinishing service, and for a reasonable fee that averages about a dollar per picture, Kodak returns your photographs on a Photo CD disc.

Each picture is stored in five different resolutions on the Photo CD: wallet (128 pixels by 192 pixels), snapshot (256 by 384), standard (512 by 768), large (1024 by 1536), and poster (2048 by 3072). Only the first three are practical for presentation graphics now, but when projection resolutions increase, you will appreciate having your images already digitized at the larger sizes.

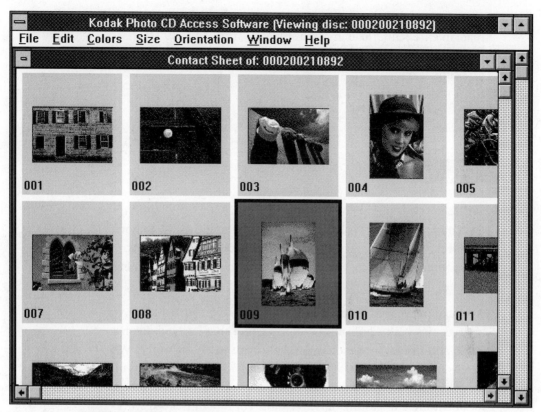

FIGURE 27.5

Kodak's *Photo CD Access Software* has a contact sheet metaphor. Used by permission of Eastman Kodak Company.

To view the pictures, you insert the disc into your CD-ROM player. Figure 27.5 shows how Kodak's *Photo CD Access Software* uses a contact sheet metaphor that lets you select a picture for full-screen viewing by clicking on one of the miniatures. You can edit the photos by cropping or changing the size, color settings, and orientation. You can copy an original or edited photo onto the clipboard as a bitmap, or you can export it in variety of image formats, including BMP and PCX. Although the pixel ratio of the exported images does not match the grid on your computer screen, the PODIUM software automatically centers the Photo CD pictures during a presentation.

Persons interested in using Kodak's Photo CD technology should read an excellent article in *MacWorld* by Martin (July, 1993) that gives detailed information about the process and provides tips for first-time users.

Waveform Editors

Windows 3.1 comes with an accessory called *Sound Recorder* that lets you record and play back waveform audio. Figure 27.6 shows how it has play, stop, record, rewind, and fast-forward buttons, plus a window that lets you view the waveshape of the incoming audio signal.

As noted in the tutorial in Part Two of this book, PODIUM for Windows comes with a built-in waveform editor that lets you digitize audio and store it in waveform audio format in files with the .WAV extension. While PODIUM lets you insert and delete segments of WAV files, it is not meant for complex audio editing that involves a lot of cutting and pasting of waveforms. For more involved work

FIGURE 27.6
Microsoft Windows *Sound Recorder*. Used by permission of Microsoft Corporation.

you need a more complete audio editor.

A good audio editor for use with PODIUM for Windows is *Sound Impression for Windows* by DigiVox Corporation. It lets you record and edit waveform files; apply echo, pan, cross-fade, chorus, and flange effects; and fine-tune waveform files with pitch, gain, noise filter, split, reverse, and merge tools. You can open up to 16 waveform editors and cut and paste between sessions. Positioning waveform files on a time line and clicking on a merge button combines them into a single sound track.

Figure 27.7 shows how *Sound Impression* has an on-screen "main component rack" based on a home stereo metaphor. Components include a mixer that controls volume and balance, a wave recorder that can record and play back waveform audio files, a MIDI player that can sequence and play MIDI files, and a CD player that can play back audio compact discs.

MIDI Sequencer/Editors

A computer program that records what you play on a MIDI keyboard and lets you edit and play back the sequence of MIDI data that was recorded is called a sequencer. The sequence of MIDI data is recorded on tracks. You can record many tracks (as many as 256) and mix them for playback as desired. There are many MIDI sequencers that let you create MIDI sequences for your PODIUM for Windows presentations; recommended programs are described in the next sections.

Band-in-a-Box

An automatic accompaniment program from PG Music called *Band-in-a-Box* is one of the more popular MIDI programs because it is great for jamming. It combines a melody sequencer with an automatic accompaniment generator that can create dozens of styles, such as hard rock, blues, and new age. *Band-in-a-Box* lets you create your own styles in addition to using the patterns that

FIGURE 27.7
DigiVox's *Sound Impression* components include a mixer, waveform
recorder, MIDI player, and CD audio player. Used by permission of
DigiVox.

ship with it. Figure 27.8 shows how you enter a sequence of
chords, pick a style, and press PLAY to make *Band-in-a-Box* generate an accompaniment of bass, drums, piano, guitar, and strings.

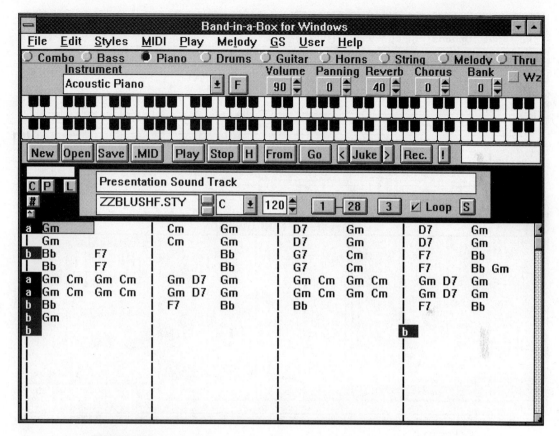

FIGURE 27.8

Band-in-a-Box's MIDI automatic accompaniment program. Used by permission of PG Music Inc.

Music generated this way is free of copyright; you can use it without restrictions in your presentations.

MidiSoft Recording Session

MidiSoft Recording Session is a Windows application that is very easy to use because of its graphical tape recorder controls. Anyone who knows how to work a tape recorder can use this program to record and play back MIDI sequences. Figure 27.9 shows how it notates automatically anything you play.

Midisoft Studio for Windows is a more fully featured professional music sequencer of which *Midisoft Recording Session* is a subset.

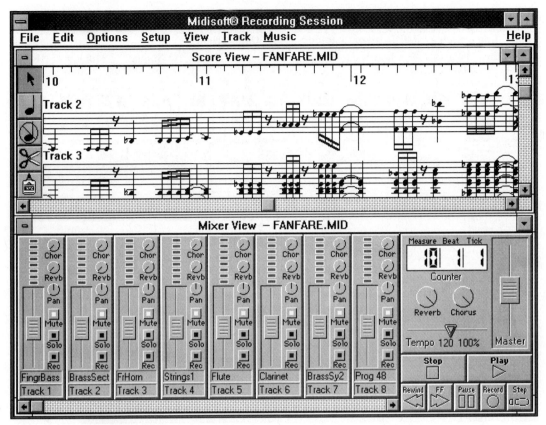

FIGURE 27.9
MidiSoft Recording Session's MIDI sequencer/editor. Used by permission of MidiSoft Corporation.

Users who learn *Recording Session* and want to progress to more advanced MIDI sequencing will find *Studio for Windows* compatible with what they have learned so far.

Power Chords

Most MIDI programs are based on piano keyboard metaphors. A Windows program from Howling Dog Systems called *Power Chords* uses a guitar interface that will appeal to users who play the guitar. Figure 27.10 shows how you click on an on-screen guitar fingerboard to create chords, copy them to a chord palette, and paste them into a song. If you do not like the voicing of a particular

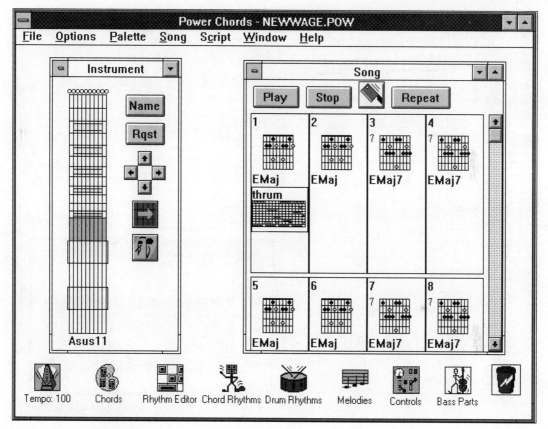

FIGURE 27.10
Creating MIDI sequences with a guitar fingerboard in *Power Chords*.
Used by permission of Howling Dog Systems.

chord, *Power Chords* will revoice it and show the new guitar finger-
ing. You can strum the chord by dragging your mouse across the
strings. You can even bend the notes, just like on a real guitar.

Cakewalk

Twelve Tone Systems' *Cakewalk* is one of the most popular MIDI
sequencers. It is available both in DOS and Windows versions.
Both are easy to use; even the DOS version has a menu bar that
makes it easy to explore *Cakewalk's* many features.

Figure 27.11 gives you an idea of why so many professional musicians use *Cakewalk Professional for Windows*. You can view and edit

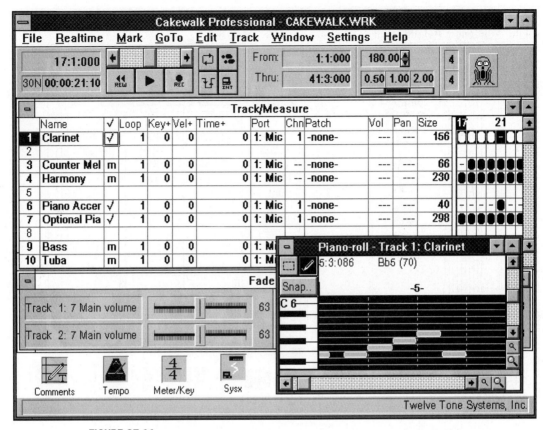

FIGURE 27.11
Cakewalk for Windows, the most popular MIDI sequencer/editor.
Used by permission of Twelve Tone Systems, Inc.

MIDI notes in piano roll, staff notation, or event list windows. It
features 256 tracks with independent looping, multiple window
editing, and videotape-to-MIDI synchronization. It even lets you
include Windows MCI multimedia commands in your MIDI
sequences.

Videodisc Mastering

In the 1980s it cost thousands of dollars to have a videodisc pressed, and you had to wait weeks or months to get it. Now there are production houses that will make a disc for as little as $300; if you pay for express mailing, you can often have it back the next day.

Videodiscs hold 54,000 slides or 30 minutes of video with a stereo sound track. To make a videodisc, you edit onto videotape the exact sequence of stills and motion sequences you want on your videodisc; then you send the videotape to the production house where it is transferred onto a videodisc. Make sure the size and format of your videotape meet the requirements of the production house.

If you need several copies of a videodisc, you may want to make a master from which copies can be pressed inexpensively. The master will cost about $2,000 per side, and copies will range in price from $10 to $20, depending on the quantity. You can see that with the 54,000 slides a videodisc holds, for the price this is the most economical way to store slides that can be accessed and displayed quickly during your presentations.

Chapter 28

Projection Alternatives

Depending on lighting conditions, the size of your audience, and the degree of portability required, you may spend more money on projecting the video from your computer than on the system unit and multimedia peripherals you put in it. This chapter discusses projection alternatives and guidelines for deciding which one best fits your needs and budget.

LCD Panels

LCD stands for liquid crystal display. LCD projection panels are flat see-through screens that fit on an overhead projector and connect to your computer's video output. As your computer turns pixels on and off, the liquid crystal responds instantly, copying the grid

FIGURE 28.1
Close-up view of an LCD panel. Photo provided courtesy of InFocus, manufacturer of the panel.

of dots from your computer screen onto the LCD panel through which the overhead projector shows your image. Liquid crystal displays used to be too slow for motion video. The newer active matrix panels are quite fast and have no problem keeping up with animated graphics and full-motion video. Figure 28.1 shows an LCD panel close up, and Figure 28.2 shows one being used in a presentation.

Some LCD panels have a problem of leaking light. When you place an LCD panel atop your overhead projector, there may be a gap between the panel and the overhead projector. Light can leak through the gap and interfere with the projected image. To fill the gap so that no light leaks, you can use masking tape or a folded piece of paper. Fold the paper in thirds as if you were going to put it in an envelope; tuck the bottom fold under the LCD panel so the other two folds cover the gap. If your overhead projector leaks light from other places, cover them also. Do not cover air vents that prevent overheating.

FIGURE 28.2
An LCD panel in use during a presentation. Photo provided courtesy of nView, manufacturer of the panel.

You must have a darkened room to use an LCD panel. Overhead fluorescent lights or daylight shining through windows will be too bright for the LCD image to be seen. The darker you make the room, the better the image will appear. If you have incandescent lighting on dimmers, you will be able to turn them on dimly. By adjusting the dimmers, you will discover the brightness threshold at which the light begins to interfere with your audience's ability to view the projected image. Incandescent lighting just below this threshold creates a nice ambience for your audience and enables note taking.

LCD panels range in price from $1,500 to $8,000. The price is influenced by the number of colors they can show, whether they can project video as well as computer input, how many simultaneous inputs can be connected, and whether they have an active or passive matrix. Active matrix panels have transistors in the pixel grid to respond quickly to mouse movements, animations, and full-motion video. Passive matrix panels have the electronics in the frame around the panel and do not react well to fast movement, which blurs the projected image.

LCD Projectors

LCD projectors resolve several problems inherent in LCD panels. LCD projectors use the same liquid crystal as LCD panels, except that instead of requiring an overhead projector, they combine the light source and the liquid crystal in the same unit. This eliminates the problem of light leaking from LCD panels. LCD projectors also tend to have an audio amplifier and speakers built-in, making them highly portable. All you need for your presentation is your computer, the LCD projector, electrical power, and a screen. Figure 28.3 shows how portable LCD projectors are.

Like LCD panels, LCD projectors are very sensitive to lighting levels. In order for your audience to view the projected image, the room must be darkened.

LCD projectors cost more than LCD panels, ranging in price from $6,000 to $12,000. If you can afford the added cost, you will be glad you did when you find out how much easier they make portable multimedia setups.

FIGURE 28.3
An LCD projector with a carrying handle for portability.
Photo provided courtesy of nView, manufacturer of the
projector.

RGB Projectors

RGB projectors have three video guns that project the colors red,
green, and blue, hence the abbreviation RGB. Each gun must be
focused and converged to match the output of the other guns. The
process of converging an RGB projector is tedious and takes a
skilled technician 15 to 30 minutes to complete.

The advantage of using RGB projectors is that they produce better
color than LCD panels. Depending on the model you buy, they can
also project a brighter image.

Figure 28.4 shows a close-up view of an RGB projector. Because
the three guns in an RGB projector contain small CRTs (cathode

FIGURE 28.4
Close-up view of an RGB projector. Photo
provided courtesy of SONY, manufacturer
of the projector.

ray tubes), RGB projectors are sometimes referred to as CRT projectors. Figure 28.5 shows how a projector lift can be used to con-
ceal a ceiling-mounted projector when it is not being used by lift-
ing the projector up into the ceiling.

While RGB projectors are sometimes used for on-location remote
setups, they are more appropriate for fixed installations where you
ceiling mount a projector permanently in a presentation room. If
you do take an RGB projector on the road, you will need to consider the added weight (50 to 100 pounds) and the time and skill
required to focus and converge it.

Not all RGB projectors can display computer images. For example,
the RGB projectors used in pizza parlors and sports bars typically
display video only and cannot be used for computer graphics. So-
called multiscan, multisync projectors can display video, data, and
computer graphics. Depending upon the brightness and size of the
projected image, RGB projectors range in price from $8,000 to
$25,000.

FIGURE 28.5
An RGB projector mounted in a ceiling lift that conceals it when not in use. Photo provided courtesy of Draper, manufacturer of the lift.

Light Valves

Light valve technology produces the brightest image for computer and video projection. It uses a metal halide or xenon arc lamp as its light source, just like the projectors in movie theaters. The resulting image is so bright and clear you can have a moderate amount of room light and your audience will still be able to see the video.

As you might expect, the best costs the most. Depending on brightness and picture size, light valve projectors range in price from $20,000 to $250,000. Most often used for permanent installations in large classrooms and auditoriums, it is possible to set them up temporarily in remote locations. They are, however, rather heavy, typically weighing more than 150 pounds.

Figure 28.6 shows a light valve projector in use; notice the amount of room lighting it can tolerate.

FIGURE 28.6
A light valve projector displaying a presentation with room lights on. Used by permission of BARCO, Inc.

Projection Screens

No matter what projector you choose, you will need a projection screen for your audience to view your presentation. There are two main types of screens: flat and curved.

Flat

Most projection screens are flat. When images are projected onto screens from the same side the audience is on, in a so-called front-screen projection, the screens are made of large sheets of white fabric on which the audience views the image. When the projector is located behind the screen for rear-screen projection, the screen consists of a flat piece of rear-screen projection fabric or glass. As the projector shines the image from behind the screen, the glass catches it, and the audience views the image on the front side of the screen.

Front-screen projection requires a darkened room; rear-screen projection lets you have some of the room lights on because they do not interfere with the projection that occurs behind the screen.

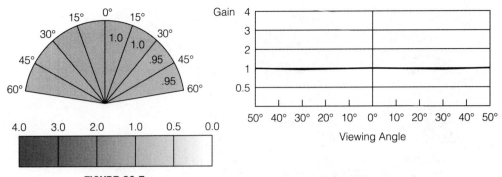

FIGURE 28.7
Brightness and viewing angle of a plain matt white projection
screen. Illustration provided courtesy of Draper Shade and Screen
Company.

Curved

Curved screens are sometimes used with RGB projectors because
they match the optical characteristics of CRTs better than flat
screens. Curved screens also boost the light level of the projected
image by focusing the reflected light into a restricted viewing
angle, typically 45 degrees from the center of the screen.

High-Gain

Both front- and rear-projected screens can be ordered with high-
gain surfaces that boost the light by a factor of two to four times;
the resulting image is two to four times brighter than the image
projected onto a regular screen. High-gain screens are especially
appropriate for multimedia because they compensate for the mar-
ginal brightness of LCD and RGB projectors. They are also cost
effective when compared to the higher price of a brighter projector. For example, instead of spending $10,000 more for a projector
that is twice as bright, you can install a high-gain screen that
boosts the light by a factor of three for just a few hundred dollars
more than the cost of a conventional screen.

High-gain screens restrict the viewing angle at which you can see
the projected image. For example, Figures 28.7 and 28.8 compare
the brightness and viewing angle of a plain matt white finish with
a Draper Reflex 4000, which was designed specifically for LCD and

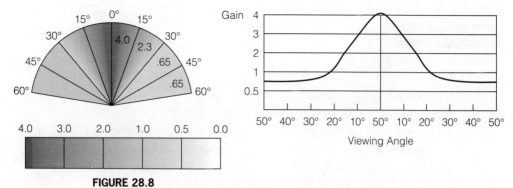

FIGURE 28.8
Brightness and viewing angle of a Reflex 4000 projection
screen. Illustration provided courtesy of Draper Shade and
Screen Company.

video projection. When you use high-gain screens, you must position them so your audience will be seated within the viewing
angle.

TV Monitors

If you are on a tight budget and cannot afford video overlay boards
or computer projection equipment, consider the possibility of using
a television set with a computer-controlled videodisc player.
Videodisc players with RS-232 serial ports for computer control can
be purchased for as little as $700, and most schools already have
television sets that can be connected to videodisc players. With
PODIUM the teacher could use a computer to navigate through
lesson plans and trigger videodisc slides and motion sequences that
students view on television sets. Although this is the least expensive method of using PODIUM, it is instructionally valid and can be
highly effective.

Before you invest in computer projection equipment, ask yourself if you really need to project your presentation, or is your audience small enough to view it on a large-screen RGB monitor. No matter how good your projector is, you will inevitably lose resolution and experience color loss when you project your presentation. You also need to be careful about lighting because lights interfere with the projected image. On the other hand, RGB monitors display your presentation with the same high resolution and beautiful colors you see on your computer screen, and you can have the room lights on.

Multiscan, multisync RGB monitors can display a wide range of computer images. When this book was printed, the list price of a 35-inch RGB monitor was about $7,000. Depending on the seating arrangement, you will need one for every 30 people in your audience. If you need more than one monitor, make sure the model

FIGURE 28.9
A 37-inch RGB monitor used in a presentation with room lights on. Photo provided courtesy of Mitsubishi, manufacturer of the monitor.

you purchase has RGB outputs as well as inputs so you can loop your presentation through the first monitor into the second. If your monitor does not have a VGA input, you will also need a VGA-to-RGB interface, which will cost about $250.

Computer Projection Comparison Matrix

Table 28.1 contains a computer projection comparison matrix that will help you decide which type of projector best fits your needs and budget.

Greenfield (1993) provides a comprehensive summary of projection system products, telling how projectors are expected to become more capable and decline in cost. New models appear almost monthly. The best place to shop for a computer projector is at the annual INFOCOMM conference, which hosts a video projection shoot-out that all of the computer projection vendors attend. Figure 28.10 shows how the vendors set up their projectors in a large exhibit hall and connects them to a video computer output provided by the INFOCOMM conference. You can walk around and compare how each projector performs while projecting that output, which cycles through still images at different resolutions, full-motion video, animations, and test slides that demonstrate the finer points of each projector.

Table 28.2 contains a matrix identifying the vendors who exhibited at INFOCOMM 1993 and the types of projectors they demonstrated. If you are unable to attend the INFOCOMM conference, contact the video distributors nearest you. They can tell you about regional conferences and exhibits at which computer projectors are shown. They may also be willing to visit your site and demonstrate different projectors, letting you compare how well your own applications project.

TABLE 28.1 Computer Projection Comparison Matrix

	LCD Panel	LCD Projector	RGB Projector	Light Valve Projector	TV Set	RGB Monitor
Portability Factor	Yes but requires overhead projector	Most	Not Very	Not Very	Somewhat	Somewhat
Focus Time	Very Fast	Fastest	30 minutes	30 minutes	None	None
Skill Required	Anyone	Anyone	Technician	Technician	Anyone	Anyone
Brightness in Lumens	200-400 depending on overhead	200-500	300-900	2000-5000	N/A	N/A
Cost Range	$1.5K-$8k	$6K-$12K	$8K-$25K	$20K-$250K	$300-$700	$3K-$7K
Room Lighting	Darkened	Darkened	Dim	Ambient	Lit	Lit
Best Size Audience	20-30	30-200	50-1500	1000-5000	30 each	30 each

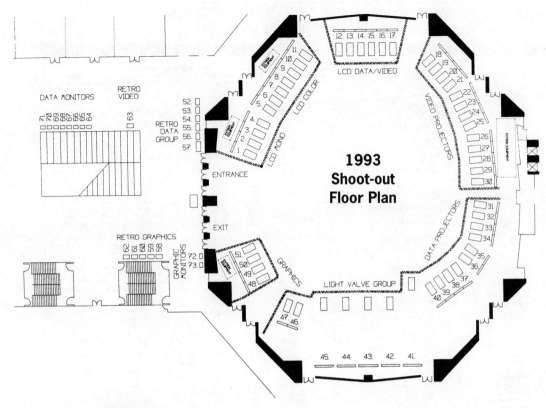

FIGURE 28.10
Floor plan of the 1993 INFOCOMM video projection shoot-out.
Provided courtesy of INFOCOMM International.

TABLE 28.2 Vendors Competing in the INFOCOMM 1993 Shoot-out. Provided courtesy of INFOCOMM International.

#	Manufacturer	Model Number	LCD Category	List Price	Booth #	H (kHz)	Active Display Area WxH	Max. Operating Temperature	Light Source	Power
1	Proxima Corporation	Multimode II	Mono	$1,595	1941	Data	7.9"x5.3"	45° C	OHP	50 Watts
2	In Focus Systems, Inc.	1600GS	Mono	$1,695	155	14-36	8.3"x6.2"	45° C	OHP	10 Watts
3	Telex Communications, Inc.	MagnaByte 5090	Mono	$1,795	947	15.75-35	8"x6"	30° C	OHP	15 Watts
4	Davis A/S	Transview Multishade	Mono	$1,895	2302	15-35	8.8"x5.9"	45° C	OHP	n/a
5	Davis A/S	Transview STN Colour	Color	$3,895	2302	15-35	7.8"x5.8"	40° C	OHP	n/a
6	Apollo	IM-24K	Color	$3,995	343	Data	6.9"x5.3"	45° C	OHP	20 Watts
7	Telex Communications, Inc.	MagnaByte 1000	Color	$3,995	947	31.5-35	8"x6"	50° C	OHP	15 Watts
8	nView	ViewFrame, Spectra C	Color	$4,495	1623	15-32	6.7"x5.1"	40° C	OHP	20 Watts
9	Sharp Electronics Corporation	QA-1150	Color	$4,995	421	15.7-35	6.7"x5.1"	30° C	OHP	20 Watts
10	Proxima Corporation	Ovation 810	Color	$4,995	1941	Data	6.7"x5.1"	50° C	OHP	50 Watts
11	NovaCorp (ASK)	Impact 16.7	Color	$6,845	1918	Data	8.2"x6.2"	30° C	OHP	15 Watts
12	In Focus Systems, Inc.	System 3000	Data/Video	$5,495	155	14-36	8.3"x6.2"	45° C	OHP	10 Watts
13	Telex Communications, INc.	MagnaByte SC-V	Data/Video	$5,995	947	31.5-35	8"x6"	50° C	OHP	15 Watts
14	Sharp Electronics Corporation	QA-1650	Data/Video	$6,495	421	15-35	8"x6"	30° C	OHP	40 Watts
15	Davis A/S	Transview Multicolor	Data/Video	$6,790	2302	15-35	7.9"x6.2"	50° C	OHP	n/a
16	nView	MediaPro	Data/Video	$6,995	1623	15-36	8.2"x6.2"	40° C	OHP	37 Watts
17	Proxima Corporation	Ovation A822C	Data/Video	$7,995	1941	Data	8.3"x6.2"	60° C	OHP	50 Watts

#	Manufacturer	Model Number	Category	List Price	Booth #	H (kHz)	V (Hz)	Light Source	Power
18	Apollo	AVP-400	Video	$2,725	343	15.7	60	LCD	380 Watts
19	Image Amplification	UltraVision 7051	Video	$3,095	2102	15-19	50-60	7" CRTs	360 Watts
20	General Electric PDPO	Geovista LCD12	Video	$3,599	1656	15.75	60	160 Watt Metal Halide	230 Watts
21	Sharp Electronics Corporation	XGH 400U	Video	$4,495	421	15.7	60	150 Watt Metal Halide	215 Watts
22	EIKI	LC-300	Video	$4,795	1331	15.75	60	160 Watt Metal Halide	250 Watts
23	Sanyo	PCL 200NX	Video	$5,350	2217	15.7	60	160 Watt Metal Halide	230 Watts
24	Sony Corporation of America	VPH 1000Q	Video	$5,490	1121	15.75	60	5.5" CRTs	230 Watts
25	Mitsubishi	VS-1202	Video	$7,200	921	15.7	60	7" CRTs	300 Watts
26	In Focus Systems, Inc.	TVT-6000	Video	$7,495	155	15.75	60	LCD	200 Watts
27	Harman Video	Series II/Model 6	Video	$7,995	2201	15.75	50-60	7" CRTs	300 Watts
28	BARCO	Barcovision 700	Video	$8,565	1255	15,30-36	37-140	7" CRTs	300 Watts
29	Panasonic	PT-B1010	Video	$9,000	443	15,31.5,33.7	50/60	CRTs	300 Watts
30	Ampro	4000V	Video	$16,995	937	15-17	30-150	9" CRTs	600 Watts
31	Panasonic	PT-200	Data	$8,000	443	15-37	50-100	7" CRTs	350 Watts
32	Harman Video	Series II/DPM-6	Data	$9,995	2201	15-37	50-80	7" CRTs	300 Watts
33	nView	Luminator	Data	$9,995	1623	15-36	50/70	Metal Halide Lamp	500 Watts
34	Mitsubishi	VS-1250R	Data	$10,900	921	15-36	50-90	7" CRTs	300 Watts
35	NEC Technologies, Inc.	Multisync 6PG	Data	$11,995	2119	15-61	38-150	7" CRTs	430 Watts
36	Electrohome Ltd.	ECP 3100	Data	$12,995	833	15-55	45-120	7" CRTs	450 Watts
37	General Electric PDPO	Imager 601	Data	$12,995	1656	15-61	38-150	7" CRTs	696 Watts
38	Sony Corporation of America	VPH-1251Q	Data	$12,990	1121	15-58	38-150	7" CRTs	440 Watts
39	Ampro	2000D	Data	$13,995	937	15-58	40-150	7" CRTs	600 Watts
40	BARCO	Barcodata 800	Data	$14,295	1255	15-58	37-140	8" CRTs	400 Watts
41	BARCO	Barcodata 5000 LC	L-Valve/Data	$42,995	1255	15-36	50-70	Metal Halide Lamp	850 Watts
42	Ampro	7000D	L-Valve/Data	$44,995	937	15-64	50-120	Metal Halide Lamp	1250 Watts
43	Hughes/JVC Technology Corp.	1500	L-Valve/Data	$44,995	1919	15-90	45-120	Xenon Arc Lamp	3600 Watts
44	General Electric PDPO	Talaria Super MLV	L-Valve/Data	$169,980	1656	15-36	50-100	Xenon Lamp	3480 Watts
45	Hughes/JVC Technology Corp.	2500	L-Valve/Graph	$59,995	1919	15-90	45-120	Xenon Arc Lamp	3600 Watts
46	NEC Technologies, Inc.	Multisync 9PG	Graphics	$18,995	2119	15-90	38-150	7" CRTs	500 Watts
47	General Electric PDPO	Imager 901	Graphics	$19,295	1656	15-90	38-150	7" CRTs	804 Watts
48	Sony Corporation of America	VPH 1271Q	Graphics	$19,990	1121	15-85	38-150	7" CRTs	450 Watts
49	Ampro	2300	Graphics	$22,995	937	15-90	37-120	7" CRTs	720 Watts
50	BARCO	Barcographics 1200	Graphics	$34,995	1255	15-135	37-140	9" CRTs	600 Watts
51	Electrohome Ltd.	Marquee 9000	Graphics	$34,995	833	30-130	45-150	9" CRTs	450 Watts
52	Sony Corporation of America	RVP 400Q	R Data	$12,295	1121	15-50	38-150	5.5" CRTs	395 Watts
53	General Electric PDPO	Imager 601RP	R Data	$19,495	1656	15-61	38-150	7" CRTs	816 Watts
54	Ampro	Retro 3000D	R Data	$19,995	937	15-58	40-150	8" CRTs	600 Watts
55	Electrohome Ltd.	Retro II/ECP 3100	R Data	$20,990	833	15-55	45-120	7" CRTs	450 Watts
56	BARCO	Retrodata 800	R Data	$20,995	1255	15-58	37-140	8" CRTs	400 Watts
57	American Video Communications	Trooper 100" LCD	R Data	$69,990	665	15/31.5/35	50-60	3 LCD/Single Lens	850 Watts
58	Sony Corporation of America	RVP 6000Q	R Graphics	$22,000	1121	15-75	38-150	5.5 CRTs	530 Watts
59	Electrohome Ltd.	Retro II/ECP 4100	R Graphics	$26,990	833	15-85	45-120	7" CRTs	450 Watts
60	Ampro	Retro 2300	R Graphics	$26,995	937	15-90	37-120	7" CRTs	600 Watts
61	BARCO	Retrographics 800	R Graphics	$27,995	1255	15-90	37-140	8" CRTs	400 Watts
62	Hitachi Denshi America, Ltd.	C70-2010R	R Graphics	$99,900	2229	15-70	40-120	9" CRTs	550 Watts
63	Ampro	Retro 1200	R Video	$7,995	937	31.5	60	CRTs	n/a

#	Manufacturer	Model Number	Category	List Price	Booth#	H (kHz)	V (Hz)	Size	Dot Pitch	Power
64	Sony Corporation of America	PGM-2710	Data Monitor	$1,695	1121	31.5	60-70	27"	.74 mm	180 Watts
65	NEC Technologies, Inc.	Multisync 3PG	Data Monitor	$3,395	2119	15-38	40-100	27"	.75 mm	280 Watts
66	Panasonic	DT-2700MS	Data Monitor	$3,500	443	15-38	50-100	27"	.63 mm	n/a
67	Mitsubishi	AM-2752A	Data Monitor	$3,700	921	15-39	45-100	27"	.76 mm	230 Watts
68	BARCO	OCM-2846	Data Monitor	$3,995	1255	15-36	45-120	26"	.8 mm	150 Watts
69	BARCO	SCM-3346	Data Monitor	$5,095	1255	15-36	45-120	31"	.8 mm	160 Watts
70	Mitsubishi	AM-3151A	Data Monitor	$5,200	921	15-36	40-70	31"	.83 mm	240 Watts
71	Mitsubishi	AM-3501R	Data Monitor	$6,900	921	15-35.5	40-70	35"	.92 mm	320 Watts
72	Mitsubishi	XC-3725	Graphic Monitor	$9,999	921	24-64	40-120	35"	.85 mm	320 Watts
73	BARCO	Megagraphics	Graphic Monitor	$19,995	1255	30-78	48-80	27"	.37 mm	210 Watts

Page 4

Chapter 29

Construction Guidelines

These guidelines are intended to serve as a checklist so you do not forget something important when you work with an architect to design new construction or renovate existing facilities. If one or more of these items is omitted in planning the project, either you will end up with a facility that disappoints you and your audience, or you will have to modify it, which costs a lot more than if you design it right the first time.

Zoned Lighting

The control of lighting is so important to good computer projection that it cannot be overemphasized. Many classrooms and auditoriums have fluorescent lighting that is very bright. Fluorescent lights cannot be put on dimmers; they can only be turned on or off. If all of the lights are controlled by the same light switch, then you have only two choices: bright light or darkness. There is no in-between.

Zoned lighting solves this problem by putting the lights on different circuits and providing for each a separate light switch that lets you turn different zones on and off. For example, you might have one zone light the front of the room where the speaker is located; another zone might light the first few rows of seats, and so on. If you are designing new construction, you should always have zoned lighting. If you are renovating an existing space, you should have the electrician add it. Zone so no light shines on the projection screen during your presentation.

Think incandescent because unlike fluorescent lights, incandescents can be put on dimmers. Zoned incandescent lighting with each zone controlled by a dimmer is the best solution for computer projection. In addition to overhead lights, put indirect incandescent lighting around the perimeter of the room, with front, sides, and rear lights on separate dimmers. In auditoriums, install indirect incandescent lighting on aisle seats and put it on a separate zone. If you will require very bright lighting for certain functions, you can also install fluorescent lighting. In rooms that have both fluorescent and incandescent lighting, a useful technique is to set the zoned incandescent lights to provide the lighting you want when using your computer projector, and then turn on the fluorescent lights to provide bright light while your audience arrives and introductions are made.

It is also possible to control the lighting from your computer. Some presentation systems automatically change light levels depending on the medium you choose. However, this adds cost that is not really necessary. You can do a fine job with a few zones of fluorescent lights and dimmer-controlled incandescent zones over your audience and around the perimeter of the room.

The light switches and dimmers should be placed in a convenient location so the speaker can adjust the light levels without having to travel a long distance or bother someone in the audience to turn lights on or off. Figure 29.1 shows a recommended zoned lighting scheme, and Figure 29.2 shows the switches and dimmers that control it.

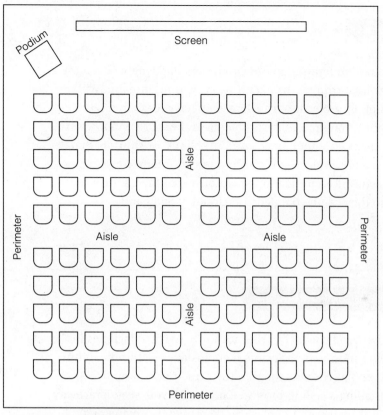

FIGURE 29.1
Zoned lighting scheme for a presentation zoom.

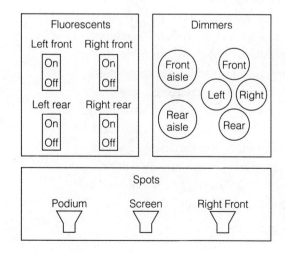

FIGURE 29.2
Zoned lighting
control panel.

Window Treatments

Planners often underestimate the brightness of daylight. Even on a cloudy day, light coming through a window is intense and will ruin a computer projection. Curtains may have leaks that let enough light through to cause problems. If there are windows in the room, make sure they have curtains, blinds, or shutters that *totally* block all incoming light; this is a must for new construction as well as renovation projects. The window treatments must be designed so they can be opened and closed quickly and easily.

Conduits, Raceways, and Datacomm

It may be hard to believe, but this author has visited facilities in which ceiling-mounted projectors were installed without conduit for the cables that connect them to the presenter's computer. If you are installing a ceiling-mounted projector, you need a raceway or conduit through which cables can be routed to a convenient location for connection to the presenter's computer.

When constructing new facilities, you can install conduit for a few hundred dollars; to add it later can cost thousands. If you are constructing a new building, make sure there are conduits or raceways through which you can pull cable into every room. Datacomm closets should be included for making and changing cable connections. While most presentations are made today via stand-alone microcomputers, networks are becoming increasingly important. You will want your presentation to be able to access last-minute corporate data from your network, as well as digital audio and video clips on the national information superhighway. For example, Elmer-Dewitt (1993) tells how the superhighway will provide instant access to television archives, TV networks, movie collections, news programs, video catalogs, and record companies.

When in doubt, put in more conduit, not less. When the University of Delaware trenched its campus to connect its academic buildings to a fiber-optic network, it put in twelve 4-inch pipes through which cables could be pulled. So far, cable has been pulled through only half of these pipes, but the added capacity will be there when needed. It cost only a few hundred dollars to add the extra pipe during construction; to add more later would cost tens of thousands.

Cabling and Connectors

Do not omit cabling in your construction or renovation budget. Practitioners have been embarrassed when they forgot about cabling and had to request additional funding to procure it. Think about all of the equipment you have, including computers, audio systems, video projectors, lights, cameras, and multimedia peripherals, and make sure you budget for the cabling and the adapters that will be needed to connect them.

Retrofitting Existing Facilities

When retrofitting existing facilities, you will have little if any control over the shape of the space. Nevertheless, here is a list of some clever modifications you can make.

1. Install a high-gain screen that will intensify the projected image. Make the screen as large as your space permits. There are too many examples of boardrooms and classrooms in which tiny screens were installed when large screens could have been used. It costs relatively little to increase the size of the screen when you are planning the renovation.

2. Follow the lighting suggestions discussed in the preceding paragraphs to supply nice, warm incandescent light that provides ambience for your audience but does not strike the projection screen during your presentation.

3. If you cannot change the room lighting and it strikes the projection screen, try installing parabolic reflector grids; they direct the light downward and reduce interference with your projected image.

4. Install a good stereo speaker system and use conduit to run the wires to a location convenient for connection to the presenter's computer. Good stereo is relatively inexpensive now, yet it adds tremendous appeal to the feel of a presentation.

5. Locate lighting and audio controls on a panel the presenter can operate without having to walk away from the multimedia computer.

6. If the audience is not large, install 35-inch RGB monitors instead of LCD or RGB projectors.

7. Make sure the audience has an unobstructed view of the presenter and the screen.

Designing New Construction

Multimedia classrooms and boardrooms can be expensive to operate. Things can go wrong during a presentation that sometimes require technical assistance. Many organizations have an audiovisual staff that provides this service. Planners designing new construction should consider ways of providing the maximum benefit for multimedia presenters without forcing the institution to add staff and incur larger ongoing costs.

A clever way to design multimedia presentation rooms without increasing ongoing costs is to construct them around a central media core. Instead of using bricks and mortar to build a wall behind the presenter, you install glass that can be used for rear-

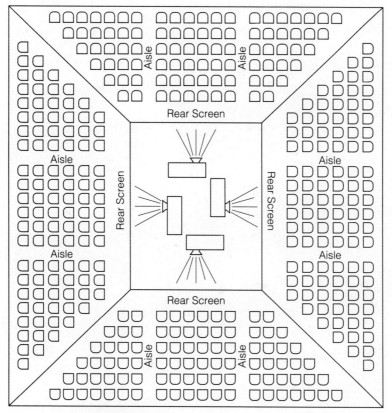

FIGURE 29.3

Floor plan for a rectangular building with a central media core.

screen projection. By locating several rooms around a central media core, you can have the rear-screen glass of each room adjoin the central core, in which the computer projectors are placed. This makes it possible for an audiovisual technician located in the central media core to handle several classrooms at once.

Figure 29.3 shows a central core design for a rectangular building, while Figure 29.4 shows a more innovative design for a circular building.

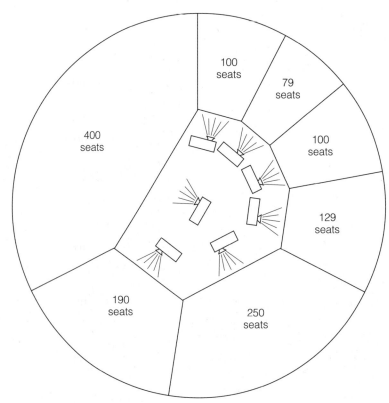

FIGURE 29.4
A circular building designed around a central media core.

Presentation Bunkers

When multimedia presentation equipment is installed permanently in a classroom or auditorium, it needs to be enclosed in cabinetry that can be secured when it is not being used. Such an enclosure is referred to as a presentation bunker.

In Chapter 30, Presentation Technology Carts, suggestions are provided for designing shelves, sizing cabinets, and positioning hardware conveniently for the presenter. These apply equally well to the design of presentation bunkers, except that because bunkers are not intended to be portable, they can be wider and do not need wheels.

There are some innovative places to visit where you can see buildings and multimedia classroom designs that illustrate the construction and renovation concepts presented in this book. By visiting these locations you will not only get ideas but also have the opportunity to ask what the designers would do differently if they could start over. Such advice can prevent costly mistakes, oversights, and needless expenditures.

University of Delware Kirkbride Lecture Hall

The University of Delaware has constructed a building specifically designed for multimedia. The Kirkbride Lecture Hall contains six classrooms and one auditorium arranged in a semicircle around a central media core. Three classrooms are on the ground floor, the auditorium is on the second floor, and three more classrooms are on the third floor. The projection equipment is located in the central media core, whence it is projected onto huge rear projection screens between the core and the classrooms.

The advantage of such a facility is that one technician working inside the core can supervise the multimedia setups for seven classrooms. The Kirkbride Lecture Hall is the most popular teaching facility on campus, and the University of Delaware is happy to arrange tours for visitors from other campuses who want to inspect it. Figure 29.5 shows the floor plan for Kirkbride Lecture Hall.

Visitors to the University of Delaware can also see the mobile multimedia technology cart that is described in Chapter 30, Presentation Technology Carts, and the Instructional Television (ITV) classrooms, which are equipped for using multimedia to create candid, classroom-videotaped courses for distance learning. A satellite uplink and fiber optics are also used for two-way interactive instructional television applications.

Florida Community College
at Jacksonville Electronic Classrooms

Jacksonville is an exciting place to visit, not only for its beautiful beaches but also because of the innovative facilities at Florida

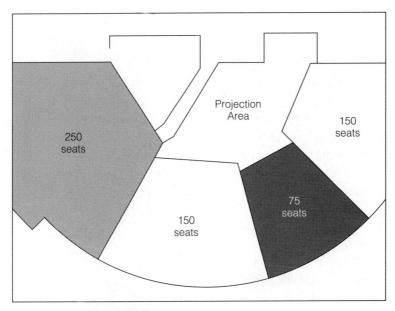

FIGURE 29.5
Kirkbride Lecture Hall with a central media core with rear-screen projection in each classroom and auditorium.

Community College at Jacksonville (FCCJ) and the University of North Florida. FCCJ has one of the nation's largest and best organized faculty development projects for using multimedia to improve classroom teaching. FCCJ has also constructed electronic classrooms that use multimedia and fiber optics to link its branch campuses. Faculty and students taking a course on one campus can interact with a class on another campus via two-way computer, audio, and video links. Large projection screens and RGB monitors provide outstanding picture quality, and surround sound makes the audio seem real. Figure 29.6 shows an interactive two-way multimedia presentation classroom. For more information about the design, cost, equipment selection, site preparation, and faculty-training model used at FCCJ, see the excellent case study by Jack Chambers (1992), who directs their Center for Academic Technology.

FIGURE 29.6
An interactive two-way multimedia classroom at Florida
Community College in Jacksonville.

University of North Florida Revolving Classrooms
Sometimes you want one large room; other times, a few smaller
spaces is what you need. The University of North Florida solved
this dilemma by constructing a large lecture hall in which sections
of the seating are on huge revolving platters that can rotate like the
floor in a revolving restaurant. To divide the lecture hall into
smaller rooms, you press a button, and the platters revolve to create three classrooms. North Florida designed this so well that no
matter which way the rooms revolve, they look like they were
designed to be that way.

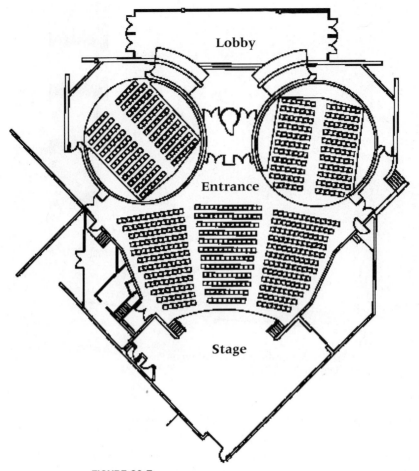

FIGURE 29.7
Revolving platter floor plan of the multimedia classrooms
at the University of North Florida.

Figure 29.7 shows the revolving platter floor plan, and Figure 29.8
shows how the main auditorium looks with its left platter revolved
to create one smaller classroom. When the right platter turns, the
seats in the upper right revolve to create a second classroom.

FIGURE 29.8
How the main auditorium looks when the left platter
revolves to partition off one classroom.

Construction Checklist

Table 29.1 summarizes this discussion by providing a checklist of
construction items to consider when renovating or building new
multimedia facilities. These are in addition to the normal guidelines for designing classrooms and lecture halls, which have been
codified by Allen (1991) in his excellent manual entitled *Design of
General-Purpose Classrooms and Lecture Halls.*

TABLE 29.1 Multimedia Construction and Renovation Checklist

Lighting

- ☐   Zoned flourescent lights
- ☐   Zoned incandescents on dimmers
- ☐   Parabolic reflector grids
- ☐   Indirect aisle lights in auditoriums
- ☐   Lighting control panel located convenient to presenter in the presentation bunker
- ☐   Curtains, blinds, or shutters on windows

Sound

- ☐   Stereo sound system
- ☐   Mixer for connecting multiple sound sources
- ☐   Lapel microphone for the presenter's voice
- ☐   Amplification controls located in the presentation bunker

Cabling

- ☐   Conduits, raceways, and datacomm closets
- ☐   Cables that will connect all multimedia components
- ☐   Adapters to make the cables fit the connectors on your multimedia devices
- ☐   Video and network connections located in the presentation bunker
- ☐   When in doubt, install more conduit, not less

Screens

- ☐   Surface for front-screen or rear-screen projection
- ☐   Use high-gain screen to intensify computer projection
- ☐   Make screen as large as room permits
- ☐   Seat audience inside high-gain screen's viewing cone
- ☐   Use 35-inch RGB monitors instead of projector if the room is small

Spaces

- ☐   Position bunker so the presenter can be seen without obstructing the audience view of the screen
- ☐   Construct presentation spaces around a central media core
- ☐   Visit sites constructed by others and ask what they would do differently

Chapter 30

Presentation Technology Carts

T he March 1993 issue of *Tech Trends* featured the University of Delaware's mobile presentation technology cart and included an article about it (Hofstetter *et al.*, 1993). The text that follows is an updated version of that article.

The University of Delaware's Instructional Technology Center developed a mobile presentation cart that enables instructors, presenters, and lecturers to deliver multimedia materials anywhere on campus. Presentations can incorporate state-of-the-art computer-controlled audio and still frames and full-motion video from a variety of sources, including videodisc, CD-ROM, read–write optical drives, and the computer's hard drive. The multimedia cart is portable enough to be moved and set up within a building by a single person and can be transported across campus. The cart includes equipment that projects the computer screen's display onto a variety of surfaces and amplifies the sound for use in large classrooms. Figure 30.1 shows the fully equipped multimedia cart open and ready for use.

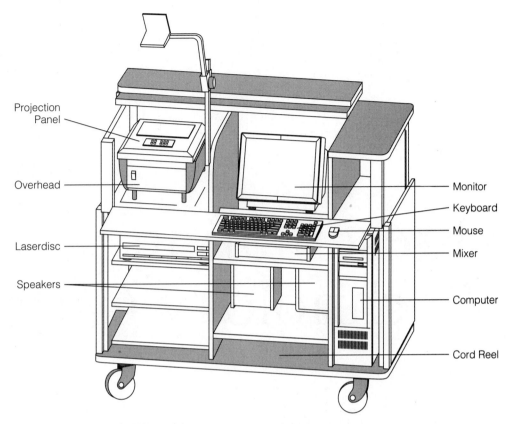

Projection Panel

Overhead

Laserdisc

Speakers

Monitor

Keyboard

Mouse

Mixer

Computer

Cord Reel

FIGURE 30.1
A fully equipped multimedia cart open and ready for use.
Original CAD drawing created by Steve Timmins; used with
permission.

Design Goals

The goal of the project was to provide a mobile presentation cart
flexible enough to accommodate a wide variety of multimedia
systems, from IBM PS/2s to the full line of Macintosh II computers. The cart needed to house a number of peripherals including
CD-ROM, videodisc, optical disk, videotape, and most important, a
high-resolution high-intensity color projection system. Hardware
included equipment for amplifying sound to large audiences and

projecting full-motion color video in classrooms. The computing equipment had to be powerful enough to run the latest multimedia software including PODIUM, *ToolBook*, Microsoft's *Video for Windows*, and Intel's DVI technology.

All of the components needed to be connected in a rugged, secure unit that could be moved not only from room to room, but also trucked across campus. Yet it needed to be as lightweight as possible to allow movement and setup within buildings by a single person. The cart had to be secure, so it could be delivered ahead of time to a classroom and left unattended without fear of misuse, theft, or vandalism. It needed to be ergonomically efficient and serve effectively as a speaker's lectern, allowing presenters to face the audience and operate the equipment in a comfortable and relaxed manner while graphics displayed on a screen behind them.

Finally, the cart had to be cost effective. Construction costs needed to be minimized without sacrificing design goals in order to make as many units as possible available for classes and presentations.

Physical Layout

Designing a structure to hold all the equipment necessary to carry out a full multimedia presentation is a relatively simple task. Designing one for maximum portability, durability and security is another matter. In addition to being able to enclose and cool the computer, audio and video systems, and other peripherals, the cart had to be narrow enough to fit through standard doorways, low enough to be seen over by any presenter, and light enough to be moved by a single person.

The depth of the cart (26 inches) was determined by taking the depth of a standard IBM PS/2 or Mac II computer (19 inches), adding 3 inches for rear access, 2 inches for the thickness of the enclosure, and 1 inch front and back for overhang so that the top and bottom rub strips, rather than the wood-paneled sides of the cart, would act as bumpers. The cart is divided into three lateral compartments: one for the overhead projector, videodisc and other internal devices; one for the monitor, mixer, and speakers; and one for the computer. The width of the cart was determined by summing the width of the computer, monitor, and maximum peripheral device width (videodisc or overhead), which totaled 51 inches including overhang. Height was determined in a similar manner, allowing 6 1/2 inches for wheels; considering presenter height and keyboard location resulted in a total height of 45 inches.

The top of the cart is constructed in three pieces. Two panels fold up and back against the top of the cart to allow for deployment of the overhead projector and viewing of the monitor, which is centrally mounted. The upper 12 inches of the front of the cart folds down to form a shelf to which the keyboard is attached and on which a mouse can be operated. This shelf is 32 inches high to accommodate a range of presenter heights. The front doors swing fully open flush against the sides of the cart, providing maximum access to the computer and peripherals. The audio mixer, located beneath the monitor, can be accessed through a space between the monitor and front shelf. An access panel 20 inches wide opens up in the back of the cart (which faces the audience) to allow for maintenance and connection without removing the peripherals; this panel has cutouts though which the speakers project sound. The doors, shelf, and top of the cart automatically lock when closed, and the rear access panel can be removed only from the inside when the cart is opened.

The interior features height-adjustable shelves for a variety of peripheral configurations and an angle-adjustable monitor shelf so differently sized monitors and presenters can be accommodated.

The cart is constructed of 3/4-inch birch plywood for a sturdy structure. The vertical surfaces are covered in a durable oak veneer, while the top and interior horizontal surfaces are covered in Formica for easy cleaning. The cart is supported by 5-inch rubber wheels on ball-bearing swivels so small obstacles such as loading ramps, molding strips, and concrete joints can be traversed with a minimum of difficulty. The cart also features durable rubber rub strips on the top and bottom surfaces to prevent damage to the finish from door frames, walls, and moving-van interiors during relocation.

The cart incorporates a number of convenience features such as a Velcro-attached keyboard, mouse holder, mouse pad, built-in cord reel, and power strips, all of which enhance the ergonomic efficiency of the assembly without appreciably increasing cost. These features make the cart truly user-friendly. Users have also noted how appealing the cart looks with its beautiful oak finish and how well it blends with traditional classroom decor.

The construction cost of the cart is in the $2,000 range, not including the computer and multimedia equipment. The weight of an empty cart is approximately 150 pounds. Fully loaded, the cart weighs 300 to 400 pounds, depending on the equipment chosen.

Equipment

The technology cart is equipped with an IBM-compatible 486 microcomputer with a large hard drive, 8 megabytes of RAM, internal CD-ROM player, video overlay card, waveform audio card, and a 15-inch color VGA monitor. This system, in conjunction with a Pioneer LD-V4400 videodisc player, runs multimedia presentation software such as PODIUM, *Multimedia Windows*, *ToolBook*, and *Storyboard Live*, as well as the full range of standard DOS applications.

The audio system consists of an audio mixer with three sets of stereo inputs connected to the waveform audio adapter, video overlay card, and videodisc player. Outputs are connected to a pair of Yamaha MS202 self-amplifying speakers. These speakers were chosen for their sturdiness, ability to produce high volumes with reasonable audio accuracy, and low cost ($300 per pair).

The cart's projection system combines a DuKane overhead projector with an nVIEW ViewFrame Spectra C projection panel. The 3,500-lumen DuKane model 663 is brighter than standard overhead projectors and features a fold-away projection lens assembly that fits neatly inside the unit while closed. The display panel was chosen because of its adaptability to different inputs (VGA or Mac II 640 by 480 graphics), high-intensity color resolution, and ability to display up to 185,193 colors. The nView unit had the best controls, color, and tint of the units tested, and featured a durable metal case and plug configuration well located for the overhead.

Improvements Made by Humber College

Humber College improved on the Delaware design by using an LCD projector instead of an overhead. Humber also put hinged doors on the back of the cart so equipment could be accessed more easily. Another improvement was adding an interior lamp to provide the presenter with indirect lighting when room lights are turned off. Figure 30.2 shows Professor Wayne Debly, who designed the Humber College cart, preparing to give a mobile presentation with PODIUM.

Future Development

The multimedia technology cart has received favorable reviews from a variety of users for its ability to project powerful multimedia presentations and standard application software under a wide range of conditions. Users are pleased with the layout of the cart's features. Small changes are being considered, such as widening the rear opening to provide better access to equipment and changing the dimensions of some of the interior shelves. One common complaint from users concerns the cart's mobility. Although it can be moved by one person, this can often be done only with considerable effort because of the cart's weight and size and the architectural features of some of the buildings where it is used. Among

FIGURE 30.2
Professor Wayne Debly with Humber College mobile presentation technology cart. Used by permission of Humber College.

solutions being considered are cutting away unnecessary parts of interior panels and using alternative construction materials (such as solid pine rather than birch plywood), which could save as much as 50% of the weight but would also make the cart substantially more difficult to construct.

However, the biggest problem is that the computer on which the user will make the presentation is locked up inside the cart. How do users get access to the computer so they can load their presentations onto it? If you load your presentation in advance, how can you be sure some interim user has not done something else to the computer that will render your presentation unworkable? The solution may be to put a portable computer docking station in place of the computer inside the cart. Then users could prepare their presentations on their own portable computers, which would dock with any technology cart containing a compatible docking station. The docking station would be prewired to all of the multimedia equipment in the technology cart, allowing users to simply slide their portable computer into the docking station, power up the equipment, and begin presenting. Figure 30.3 illustrates the docking-station concept.

As previously mentioned, the technology cart can also be used in a fixed location as a presentation bunker simply by removing its wheels. If you install a bunker in a room with a ceiling-mounted or rear-screen projector, you will not need to include a projector in the bunker. Otherwise the design criteria for carts and bunkers are similar. Table 30.1 contains a checklist of items to consider when constructing presentation technology carts and bunkers.

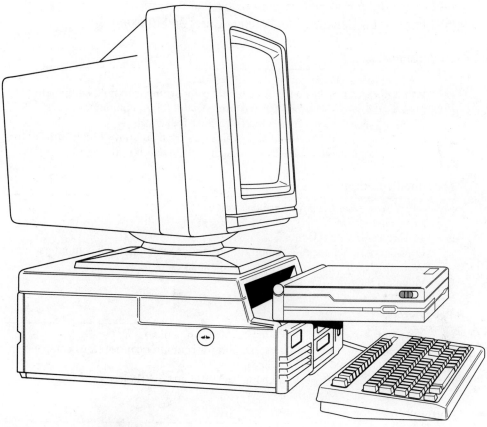

FIGURE 30.3
How a portable computer mates with a docking station that
can be preconnected to video projection and audio amplification equipment.

TABLE 30.1 Checklist for Designing Technology Carts and Bunkers

Dimensions

- ☐ Depth of cart 26 inches
- ☐ Width of cart 51 inches with three lateral compartments to hold equipment
- ☐ Shelves are height adjustable to accommodate different equipment needs
- ☐ Height 45 inches including 6.5 inch clearance for wheels
- ☐ Wheels are 5-inch rubber on ball bearing swivels; if you have rough surfaces to traverse, use inflatable wheels and design wheel wells into the cart

Multimedia Computer

- ☐ 486 processor with a large hard disk drive
- ☐ 8 megabyte RAM
- ☐ 15-inch color VGA monitor
- ☐ Consider optional docking station for presenters with notebook computers
- ☐ Waveform digital audio card (MCI compatible)
- ☐ Video overlay card (MCI compatible)

Peripherals

- ☐ CD-ROM player with audio outputs (MCI compatible)
- ☐ Videodisc player with RS-232 serial port for computer control (MCI compatible; Pioneer LD-V4400 recommended)
- ☐ S-VHS videotape player for playing back VHS and S-VHS tapes

Audiovisual

- ☐ Audio mixer with eight inputs and two outputs
- ☐ Self-amplified speakers (Yamaha MS-202 recommended)
- ☐ Optional lapel microphone for amplifying the presenter's voice
- ☐ LCD projector or LCD panel with overhead projector that has a retractable lens assembly (DuKane model 663 recommended)

TABLE 30.1 *Continued.*

Cables and adapters

☐   Cables for connecting all of the above
☐   Adapters to make the cables fit the connectors on your multimedia circuit boards and peripherals

Ergonomic

☐   Presenter must be able to face the audience while using the multimedia computer
☐   Cart or bunker must be low enough for presenter to be seen over it
☐   Pull-down shelf includes computer keyboard pre-positioned with Velcro
☐   Built-in cord reel and power strips
☐   Convenience lamp so presenter can see when lights are off
☐   Mouse pad must be movable to accommodate left-handed as well as right handed presenters
☐   Use lightweight materials to keep cart light enough to be moved by a single person
☐   Install rear access doors to make equipment readily accessible to technicians
☐   Cart or bunker locks automatically when closed
☐   Vertical surfaces covered with oak veneer; horizontal surfaces covered in Formica for easy cleaning
☐   Rub strips to protect cart from damage during transport

Chapter 31

Portable Setups

One of multimedia's most attractive features is how portable it has become. Large-scale integration has made it possible for portable notebook computers to perform tasks that used to require a desktop full of equipment. LCD projectors with internal speakers provide a way for you to show your presentation without putting a burden on your host or needing a technician to help you set up.

Adapter Cards

Depending on the content of your presentation, you may require a portable computer that has a card cage to hold adapter cards needed to present multimedia events. Attractive alternatives on the market when this book went to press include portables manufactured by IBM, Dolch, Compaq, Toshiba, NEC, and Dell.

If your presentation does not require multimedia adapter cards, you can travel with a lighter and more compact notebook computer. Most computer vendors offer models with large hard disk drives based on a 486 chip to make presentations run fast. You can also get an optional docking station, which introduces a new concept into the design of multimedia presentation facilities.

Docking Stations

Just as you slide a videotape into a VCR and play the program on it, so also can you slide your notebook into a docking station, power up, and run your multimedia software. Suppose you equip a dozen rooms in your company or school with large-screen projectors and sound systems for multimedia presentations. If you include a docking station in each room and connect it to the large-screen projector and sound system, then your presenters can simply dock their laptops, power up, and begin speaking. Any peripherals connected to the docking station will be automatically available to the presenter, including videodisc, compact disc, and network connections.

Many docking stations have a card cage; when the notebooks are docked, they can use multimedia cards in the docking station. Fortunately, docking stations are inexpensive and can be included in the design of your facilities without incurring prohibitive costs. IBM, NEC, Compaq, Apple, and ALR manufacture docking stations for their notebook computers.

Airplane Travel

It is not a good idea for airplane travelers to check as baggage the computer they plan to use in their presentation. The computer could be lost or damaged, and that would ruin your presentation. The solution to this problem is to get a hard plastic carry-on computer case that has built-in wheels to help you cart it through airports. Starr, Calzone, and Anvil manufacture cases designed to fit under the seat in front of you or in the overhead bin. These cases have aluminum tubes that can be extended to make it easy for you to cart the computer. This lets you place another case atop the computer case and wheel both easily through the airport. For example, the second case might contain your LCD projector with built-in sound amplifier and speakers. International travelers should beware that most overseas flights permit only one piece of carry-on luggage; however, business class passengers can often obtain permission for a second piece of carry-on.

Portable Setup Checklist

Table 31.1 contains a checklist for you to consider when you make portable multimedia presentations. If any of these items are missing, your presentation could fail due to setup problems. You should advise your host of any items you cannot bring that you want to have provided for you. For example, when given enough notice, your host will normally be able to provide a projection screen, a sound system, a computer monitor, an extension cord, a power strip, and an overhead projector if you need one. Make sure you mention that the room must be capable of being darkened so the audience will be able to see the projected image. If the audience is large, you will want a microphone so your voice can be heard. To free your hands for working the computer during your talk, request a lapel microphone.

TABLE 31.1 Portable Multimedia Equipment Checklist

- ☐ Portable computer
- ☐ Computer monitor for the presenter
- ☐ Computer projector for displaying the presentation
- ☐ Overhead projector if using an LCD panel
- ☐ Self-amplified speakers for sound
- ☐ Lapel microphone if audience is large
- ☐ Cables for connecting all of the above
- ☐ Adapters needed to make the cables fit the connectors
- ☐ Projection screen
- ☐ Table on which to place the presenter's equipment
- ☐ Extension cord and power strip

Chapter 32

Catalogs and Buyers' Guides

T here are several catalogs and buyers' guides that provide a comprehensive listing of new multimedia hardware and software products.

ICIA *Directory of Multimedia Equipment, Software and Services*

The International Communications Industries Association (ICIA) publishes the *Directory of Multimedia Equipment, Software and Services*. It lists more than 500 multimedia products and services. Entries include illustrations, prices, uses, features, specifications, compatibility, and vendor contact information. It also includes a directory of multimedia award winners that serves as a "Who's Who" of multimedia. For ordering information, contact the ICIA at 3150

Spring Street, Fairfax, VA 22031-2399; phone (703) 273-7200; or
FAX (703) 278-8082.

T.H.E. Journal

T.H.E. stands for Technical Horizons in Education. *T.H.E. Journal*
appears monthly; each issue contains application highlights and
dozens of new product announcements. Each year *T.H.E. Journal*
publishes the *Multimedia Source Guide*, which lists hundreds of multimedia products and tells how to order them. Subscribers also
receive special multimedia supplements from vendors like IBM,
Apple, and Zenith. *T.H.E. Journal* is free to qualified individuals in
educational institutions and training departments in the United
States and Canada. To subscribe, phone (714) 730-4011 or FAX
(714) 730-3739. The mailing address is 150 El Camino Real, Suite
112, Tustin, CA 92680.

New Media

New Media magazine is probably the best single source for keeping
up with what's new in multimedia. Like *T.H.E. Journal*, it appears
monthly and publishes an annual buyers' guide. *New Media* contains dozens of full-color pictures that illustrate the products it
describes, and the layout is visually appealing. To subscribe to *New
Media* write P.O. Box 1771, Riverton, NJ 08077-7331, or phone
(609) 764-1846. Be sure to ask about a free subscription, which is
available to qualified readers.

Multimedia Madness

A multimedia hardware and software shopper's guide appears in Ron Wodaski's (1992) book *Multimedia Madness*, which is published by Sams Publishing (ISBN 0-672-30249-7). It also includes reviews and sample screens from several multimedia presentation packages.

The Videodisc Compendium

More than 2,000 videodiscs have already been produced for use in education and training. They are cataloged in *The Videodisc Compendium*, which appears quarterly. To subscribe, contact Emerging Technology Consultants, 2819 Hamline Avenue North, St. Paul, MN 55113; phone (612) 639-3973; or FAX (612) 639-0110.

Chapter 33

Associations, Conferences, and Exhibits

T he best way to keep abreast of new developments is to join a
few key associations and attend their annual conferences and
exhibits.

AECT

AECT stands for Association for Educational Communications and
Technology; it is the largest professional association for audiovisual
and multimedia practitioners. AECT conventions are attended by

an interesting mix of media vendors, college professors, and students looking for career opportunities in communications technology. It is a highly professional organization that publishes several research journals as well as the monthly review of technology called *Tech Trends*. All members of the AECT receive *Tech Trends* automatically. To join, write the AECT at 1025 Vermont Avenue NW, Suite 820, Washington, DC, or phone the AECT office at (202) 347-7834. Their FAX is (202) 347-7839.

INFOCOMM

INFOCOMM is an annual exhibit of audiovisual and new media equipment sponsored by the ICIA. Cruising the aisles of the INFOCOMM exhibit is an excellent way of seeing the latest multimedia presentation technology. For information on upcoming INFOCOMM conferences, contact the ICIA at 3150 Spring Street, Fairfax, VA 22031-2399. Their phone is (703) 273-7200, and their FAX is (703) 278-8082.

SALT

SALT stands for Society for Applied Learning Technology. Like the AECT, SALT is a professional association that fosters careers in technology. It publishes research journals and holds annual conferences and exhibits. While the AECT is oriented more toward the education industry, SALT focuses on industrial and military-training applications. However, both the AECT and SALT hold excellent meetings for anyone dealing with media to attend.

To join SALT, write their headquarters at 50 Culpeper Street, Warrington, VA 22186, or phone the society at (703) 347-0055.

COMDEX

COMDEX is a huge exhibition of computer technology that occurs twice a year, once in the fall, and then again in the spring. The exhibit is so large that few cities have enough exhibition space to host it. Fall COMDEX is held in Las Vegas, and spring COMDEX is held in Atlanta.

COMDEX used to be attended almost exclusively by remarketers looking for products to sell, but now the majority of those attending are end users in search of computing solutions. Vendors invest a small fortune in their COMDEX booths, giveaways, and promotions. Attending COMDEX at least once is an experience anyone working with media will enjoy. For information about COMDEX, contact The Interface Group, 300 First Avenue, Needham, MA 02194-2722; telephone (617) 449-6600; or FAX (617) 444-4806.

InterMedia

The International Conference on CD-ROM and Multimedia is cohosted annually by InterMedia and *New Media* magazine. For details, phone (800) 832-3513 or write *New Media* at P.O. Box 1771, Riverton, NJ 08077-7331.

PODIUM Ordering Information and Discount Coupon

P ODIUM is published by the Instructional Technology Center at the University of Delaware. Standard pricing for individual copies, quantity purchases, and network licenses is provided in Tables A.1 and A.2. Institution-wide site licenses are negotiated on an individual basis.

If you are purchasing a single copy, you can use the coupon printed on page 225 to receive a $50 discount off the normal retail price of PODIUM. This discount is available only to purchasers of this book, and you must clip the coupon out of the book and mail the original copy to get the discount; photocopies of the coupon will not be accepted.

You may pay via purchase order or use your VISA, MasterCard, or

PODIUM DISCOUNT COUPON

This coupon entitles purchaser to a $50 discount off the normal single-copy price of PODIUM. It is for single copies only and may not be used with quantity purchases. Please fill it out and enclose it with your PODIUM order.

Single-Copy Price

Version of PODIUM
(Check one):

	Normal		Discounted	
	Educational	*Commercial*	*Educational*	*Commercial*
☐ PODIUM for DOS	$395	$595	**$345**	**$545**
☐ PODIUM for Windows	$495	$695	**$445**	**$645**
☐ PODIUM for Presentation Manager	$495	$695	**$445**	**$645**

Discover card. Credit card orders must include the type of credit card, the credit card number, the expiration date, and the cardholder's signature. All PODIUM orders should be mailed or FAXed as follows:

The Instructional Technology Center
305 Willard Hall Education Building
University of Delaware
Newark, DE 19716

FAX: (302) 831-2089
Inquiries: (302) 831-8164

TABLE A.1 PODIUM for DOS Pricing

	Educational price per copy	Commercial price per copy
One Copy	$395	$595
2–5 Copies	$295	$495
More than 5	$250	$450
More than 10	$150	$250
Network software and license for up to 20 simultaneous users	$2,000	$3,000
License for each additional 10 simultaneous users	$1,000	$1,500

TABLE A.2 Pricing for PODIUM for Windows and PODIUM for Presentation Manager

	Educational price per copy	Commercial price per copy
One Copy	$495	$695
2–5 Copies	$395	$595
More than 5	$300	$500
More than 10	$200	$300
Network software and license for up to 20 simultaneous users	$2,750	$4,000
License for each additional 10 simultaneous users	$1,375	$2,000

Installing PODIUM from Diskettes

I f your computer does not have a CD-ROM drive, you will want to find a computer that does. Most businesses, computer labs, and public libraries have one. Make sure its floppy disk drive uses diskettes that are compatible with the drive in your computer so you can use floppy disks to transfer PODIUM to your computer. Follow the instructions for the version of PODIUM you wish to install.

To move PODIUM for DOS to your computer, follow these steps. Be sure to substitute the proper drive letters in case your computer is configured differently. These instructions assume that the floppy disk drive is A, the hard disk is drive C, and the CD-ROM drive is D.

First you must back up all of the files from the PODIUM directory on the CD-ROM drive onto floppy disks. For example, suppose your CD-ROM is drive D and your floppy is in drive A. Here is what you would type:

```
backup  d:\PODIUM\*.*  a:\  /s
```

The computer prompts you when it requires more diskettes; keep them clearly labeled as PODIUM Disk 1, PODIUM Disk 2, and so on. PODIUM takes about 1.4 MB of disk space, so you want enough disks to hold that much.

To transfer PODIUM to your computer, you must first create the PODIUM directory on your hard disk drive. Assuming your hard disk drive is drive C, type the following:

```
md  c:\podium
md  c:\podium\tqm
```

Now insert PODIUM Disk 1 into your computer and restore the files into your PODIUM directory. For example, if your floppy is in drive A and you created your PODIUM directory on drive C, you would type the following:

```
restore  a:\  c:\podium\*.*  /s
```

To start PODIUM, switch to your hard drive, enter the PODIUM directory, and run PODIUM. For example, if you installed PODIUM on drive C, you would type the following:

```
cd  c:\podium
podium
```

To move PODIUM for Windows to your computer, follow these steps. Be sure to substitute the proper drive letters in case your computer is configured differently. These instructions assume that the floppy disk drive is A, the hard disk is drive C, and the CD-ROM drive is D.

First you must back up all of the files from the WNPODIUM directory on the CD-ROM drive onto floppy disks. For example, suppose your CD-ROM is drive D and your floppy is in drive A. Here is what you would type:

```
backup  d:\WNPODIUM\*.*  a:\  /s
```

The computer prompts you when it requires more diskettes; keep them clearly labeled as PODIUM Disk 1, PODIUM Disk 2, and so on. PODIUM takes about 1.4 MB of disk space, so you want enough disks to hold that much.

To transfer PODIUM to your computer, you must first create the WNPODIUM directory on your hard disk drive. Assuming your hard disk drive is drive C, type the following:

```
md  c:\wnpodium
md  c:\wnpodium\tqm
```

Now insert PODIUM Disk 1 into your computer and restore the files into your WNPODIUM directory. For example, if your floppy is in drive A and you created your WNPODIUM directory on drive C, you would type the following:

```
restore  a:\  c:\wnpodium\*.*  /s
```

Next, from your Windows Program Manager, click anywhere inside the Windows Program Group in which you want the PODIUM icon to appear. This makes it your active group.

Pull down the File menu, select New, select Program Item, and click on OK. In the Program Item Properties Description field, type PODIUM. In the Command Line field, type the following:

```
c:\wnpodium\wnpodemo.exe
```

Click on OK to close the Properties dialog.

To start PODIUM, double-click on the PODIUM icon that now appears on your Windows desktop.

PODIUM for Presentation Manager

To move PODIUM for Presentation Manager to your computer, follow these steps. Be sure to substitute the proper drive letters in case your computer is configured differently. These instructions assume that the floppy disk drive is A, the hard disk is drive C, and the CD-ROM drive is D.

First you must back up all of the files from the PMPODIUM directory on the CD-ROM drive onto floppy disks. For example, suppose your CD-ROM is drive D and your floppy is in drive A. Here is what you would type:

```
backup  d:\PMPODIUM\*.*  a:\  /s
```

The computer prompts you when it requires more diskettes; keep them clearly labeled as PODIUM Disk 1, PODIUM Disk 2, and so on. PODIUM takes about 1.4 MB of disk space, so you want enough disks to hold that much.

To transfer PODIUM to your computer, you must first create the PMPODIUM directory on your hard disk drive. Assuming your hard disk drive is drive C, type the following:

```
md  c:\pmpodium
md  c:\pmpodium\tqm
```

Now insert PODIUM Disk 1 into your computer and restore the files into your PMPODIUM directory. For example, if your floppy is in drive A and you created your PMPODIUM directory on drive C, you would type the following:

```
restore  a:\  c:\pmpodium\*.*  /s
```

Next, from your OS/2 desktop, open the Templates folder and use your right mouse button to drag a program icon onto your desktop; the new program settings display appears. In the path and filename field, type the following:

    c:\pmpodium\pmpodemo.exe

In the working directory field, type the following:

    c:\pmpodium

Finally, click on the General tab and in the title field enter the name PODIUM for PM. Double-click on the little PODIUM icon in the upper left corner of the Settings window to close it.

To start PODIUM, double-click on the PODIUM icon that now appears on your OS/2 desktop.

References

Allen, Robert L. *Design of General-Purpose Classrooms and Lecture Halls* (University Park: Penn State University-Wide Classroom Improvement Committee, 1991).

Canning, Jim. "New Multimedia Software Tools Can Help You Add Zing to Your Presentations," *InfoWorld* (June 22, 1992), 122.

Chambers, Jack; Mullins, John; Boccard, Brenda; and Burrows, David. "The Learning Revolution: Electronic Classrooms," *Interactive Learning International* (Volume 8, 1992), 291–295.

Elmer-Dewitt, Philip. "Take a Trip into the Future on the Electronic Superhighway," *Time* (April 12, 1993), 50–55.

Eiser, Leslie. "Multimedia Science Programs: Moving Science Education Beyond the Textbook," *Technology & Learning* (March, 1992), 16–30.

Emerging Technology Consultants. *The Videodisc Compendium* (St. Paul: Emerging Technology Consultants, quarterly).

Fridlund, Alan J. "Systat for Windows Has Number-Crunching Power," *InfoWorld* (May 17, 1993), 79–83.

Greenfield, Elizabeth. "Projection Systems: Products Mature While the Video Age Arrives," *T.H.E. Journal* (April, 1993), 12–18.

Hofstetter, Fred. "PODIUM: Presentation Overlay Display for Interactive Uses of Media," *Academic Computing* (November, 1989), 10–13, 48–50.

Hofstetter, Fred. "Institutional Support for Improving Instruction with Multimedia," *EDUCOM Review* (January/February, 1992), 27–30.

Hofstetter, Fred. "Making Multimedia Possible Through Word Processing," IBM Higher Education Supplement to *T.H.E. Journal* (March, 1992), 38–39.

Hofstetter, Fred. "DVI Authoring: A Tutorial for Teachers," *T.H.E. Journal* (October, 1992), 85–86.

Hofstetter, Fred; Morgan, Michael; Sine, Patricia; Timmins, Steven; and Wilson, James. "Design and Construction of a Multimedia Technology Cart for Secure, Efficient, and Cost-Conscious Classroom Use," *Tech Trends* (March, 1993), 22–24.

Martin, James A. "Hands-On: Photo CD," *MacWorld* (July, 1993), 92–97.

McCormack, Shawn P. "TQM: Getting It Right the First Time," *Training & Development* (June, 1992), 43–46.

Wodaski, Ron. *Multimedia Madness* (Carmel, IN: Sams Publishing, 1992).

Index